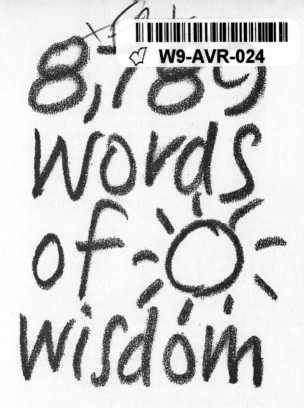

8,789
words
of ☼
wisdom

by Barbara Ann Kipfer

Illustrated by Matt Wawiorka

WORKMAN PUBLISHING, NEW YORK

Copyright © 2001 by Barbara Ann Kipfer

Illustrations © 2001 by Matt Wawiorka

All rights reserved. No portion of this book may be
reproduced—mechanically, electronically, or by any
other means, including photocopying—without written
permission of the publisher. Published simultaneously
in Canada by Thomas Allen & Son Limited.

Library of Congress Cataloging-in-Publication Data
Kipfer, Barbara Ann.
    8,789 words of wisdom / by Barbara Ann Kipfer ;
illustrated by Matt Wawiorka.
    p. cm.
    ISBN   978-0-7611-1730-8
    1. Conduct of life—Quotations, maxims, etc.
    I. Title: Eight thousand seven hundred eighty nine
words of wisdom. II. Title.
    BJ1581.2.K496
    2001 818'.5402—dc21   2001017699

Workman books are available at special discounts
when purchased in bulk for premiums and sales
promotions as well as for fund-raising or educational
use. Special editions or book excerpts can also be
created to specification. For details, contact the
Special Sales Director at the address below.

Workman Publishing Company, Inc.
225 Varick Street
New York, NY 10014-4381

www.workman.com

Printed in the United States

First printing March 2001

20 19 18 17 16

ACKNOWLEDGMENTS

This is really a "commonplace book"— a personal journal in which quotable passages, literary excerpts, and comments are written. It evolved from notes kept by me and my husband, Paul Magoulas. Paul is equally responsible for this collection, and I thank him for all of his contributions, his enthusiasm for this book, and his love.

This book is dedicated to all those people wise enough to share their guidance and to those who have brought us those words in print and other media, especially the late Sally Kovalchick, my first editor at Workman.

I would like to thank Jennifer Griffin for her terrific editing and Peter Workman for his support and for giving me the opportunity to publish this work.

To my "wise guys," Kyle Kipfer and Keir Magoulas: Thank you for the inspiration. There is no more challenging job than raising children, and for that we all need a lot of wisdom!

There are many ways to live a good life, and *8,789 Words of Wisdom* is designed to help you find which ones are right for you. It is an interactive book, intended to challenge you to interpret the meaning of your life and then to act upon that new knowledge. It is unlike other self-help books because it is not "one size fits all"; it will become something different each time you read it, according to your circumstances. One line may resonate deeply with you; whereas another line may have great significance for someone else. The lines that have meaning for you will make it your book. After all, only *you* can bring wisdom to yourself.

In many ways, the collection of wisdom here is like a poem. Each line can define a moment for you. Pick the book up and open it to any page, and you will be able to find something that appeals and applies to you. Every day can bring a new insight to your life, enabling you to take from this book what you need. Maybe you will follow the guidance of an entry just for a day, or maybe you will keep following it until it becomes a habit. Some of you will add another change the next day, and then maybe another after that. And like a poem, the book will change for you over the years. What did not apply to your life at age fifteen may have great meaning for you at age fifty.

This is a very personal book for me. Over the years I have been collecting my secrets to life improvement—great advice, formulas, wise words from great thinkers, maxims, and just plain common sense. Some of the lines are quotes, and I have tried to attribute all of them. However, as this is a collection gathered over a lifetime, many are paraphrases. I am grateful to the wise and witty contributors, from Will Shakespeare to Will Rogers. Some of the lessons here are new; others are oldies but goodies. I hope all of them make your life happier, healthier, and better in just about every way, as they have mine.

Do not disregard your
mistakes

Money is not meant to be served

Love your work, then you will find
pleasure in mastering it

Appreciate the many things that
make your life so valuable

Act the part and you will become
the part

Don't criticize others when you
are angry with yourself

Don't wait for the ideal time
to begin something

Stay on a clear course

Grab happiness in the passing
    moments of life

Keep a stash of extra batteries

Love carries great expectations

Be afraid only of standing still

Be yourself

Love always eases pain

Never underestimate the power
    of simple courtesy

Plan your work and work your plan

Never look back

Panic productively

Communicate in a way as to leave as
    little room for misunderstanding
    as possible

Trust your instincts

Don't take life or death too seriously

Converse to please others,
    not yourself

It is harder than we remember
    to be a child

Love all, trust a few, do wrong
    to none

If it looks like a duck, walks like
    a duck, and quacks like a duck,
    it is a duck

Youth's biggest mistake is its lack
    of originality

It takes money to make money

Not everything can be made sense of

Let anger die quickly

Use your dictionary

One who cannot tolerate small
    ills can never accomplish
    great things

Know the ropes

Love many things

Be patient; patience can wait
    for anything

Make decisions based on the
    whole picture

Your eyes are the windows of
    your soul

Your character is your destiny

Trust can be destroyed faster than
    it can be built

We are sometimes taken into troubled waters not to drown, but to be cleansed

What you have been taught to believe is not as important as what you know

Inspire your children to live life to the fullest

In life, some things are bigger than they look from a distance

Live in harmony with your beliefs and ideals

Avoid blaming, praising, or comparing people

Understand the difference between being at work and working

Face your fears with confidence

Education is the most important aspect of society

Get a good night's sleep

The apple doesn't fall far from its tree (Ralph Waldo Emerson)

In every fault there is folly

Help others as they help you

Hang on longer than your
   competition

Time is more important to people
   who do things

Use your memory to make your life
   more enjoyable

Something ordinary in the past
   becomes valuable in the future

Throughout history, man has
   attempted to alter his
   consciousness

He who hesitates is sometimes saved

Actively pursue the good in all the
   particulars of your daily life

Regularly examine your motives

Whatever is worth doing at all,
   is worth doing well
   (Earl of Chesterfield)

Do not pursue fame

Learning consists in daily
   accumulating

Love without expectations

The best-laid plans of mice and men
   often go astray (Robert Burns)

All questions will eventually
    be answered

Be original

Do something of your own design

Realize that there is no such thing as
    a perfect marriage

Enter into marriage knowing that it
    will not be perfect

Do not become angry with people
    who do not agree with your
    opinion

Perform acts of goodness from within

Do not become what you cannot
    stand

Believe in yourself with all your
    tenacity

Dream big

Leave nothing for tomorrow that you
    can do today

Chop your own wood; it will warm
    you twice

Parts of life are left to chance

Most things in life are taken
    for granted

You can never go wrong keeping your
  mouth shut

There is no time like the present

The important thing is not the
  triumph but the struggle

Never hate the truth

Enjoy what you have; let the fool
  hunt for more

Comedy is all about timing

Leave them laughing

Believe in the goodness of others

A person is not deceived by others,
  he deceives himself

Put your mind in gear before you put
  your tongue in action

You do not know you've learned
  something until after the fact

Remain open, flexible, curious

Visualize better days ahead

Solve problems instead of making
  them worse

Be the solution

Love books

Read as much as you can

It isn't what you do,
   it's the way you do it

Let the world come to you

Don't make commitments you don't
   plan to keep

Remember the lessons you've learned

Sometimes things that hurt, teach

Teaching someone to do something is
   like relearning it yourself

The innocent bystander often gets
   beaten up

You cannot have enough ideas

Every calamity is a spur to action

Worry about today before tomorrow

The young should love life like
   the old

Live each day as if it were your last

When you believe in something, you
   become eloquent

It is loving and giving that make life
   worth living

Rear and nourish children with
kindness

A lover's faults cannot bother you

Mind your own business

Why worry?

Understand what you know

Your greatest contribution to the
sum of things is yourself

Any plan that cannot be changed is
a bad one

Yesterday will never come again,
but you have today

All new fashions eventually become
old

If you buy happiness on installment,
the payments last much longer
than the happiness

He who laughs, lasts

Respond to rudeness with kindness

Love many, hate few

Learn to paddle your own canoe

If you can pull your own weight,
you can pull 5 percent more

Men and women may be different
from each other, but their souls
can still be combined to form one

Always make your bed

Nurture your friendships

Show your good manners by putting
up pleasantly with bad ones

Weakness breeds evil

A teacher's job is to make his/her
students smarter than he/she

To the ant, a few drops of rain is
a flood

Nature is imitated by art

You will always be able to clothe
yourself, if you know how to sew

Remember where you came from

Listen with your eyes

Willpower is the ultimate power

Understand more than you can
explain

Envy and fear are the major cause
of hatred

You're as young as you feel

Chew everything thirty-two times

You must run to win the race

Every day is a clean slate

Scribble down your thoughts
as you have them

Personality opens doors;
character keeps them open

When you really like someone,
tell them

Let experience guide you

Forgive and forget

No person experiences an emotion
that has not already been felt by
someone else

Everyone is an amateur at death

Dreams should always be optimistic

Getting mad seldom helps your cause

Lying is usually more difficult than
telling the truth

Leading with your chin can be
painful

Don't mind if others don't share
your convictions

Order makes for peace

The truth is more powerful than a lie

Be curious and ask why a lot

Your health is affected by whether
you learn to forgive or not

It is better to live happy than to
die sad

Never let them see you sweat

Do not be ashamed to fail

You can be someone who can be loved

Love, friendships, and opportunities
never occur when judgment is
made on appearance alone

Don't be afraid to ask for help

Don't criticize, condemn, or complain

Look back at your ancestors for
strength

What is useful will last; what is
hurtful will sink

Honor is sought by others to confirm
it in ourselves

Do not disparage your competitor

Listening to someone is sometimes
all the help he needs

The purpose of schools is to teach
how to become self-educated

Know more about yourself than other
people know about you

Surround yourself with people who
are more intelligent than you are

You have to take the rough with
the smooth

Don't apologize for being early

Never lose your child heart

You have two ears and one mouth;
use them in the same proportion

The truth can come out at the
wrong time

Do what matters most at the time

If you know nothing, say nothing

Honesty is an ongoing process

Move forward, not backward

All people are born free and equal

Explore your relationships

A lie is a lie to yourself

People change and forget to tell
each other

Don't talk about being tired

No revenge is ever worthwhile

Silence is the hardest argument
to refute

From the sublime to the ridiculous is
but a step (Napoléon Bonaparte)

Practice ethics 24 hours a day, 7 days
a week, 365 days a year

Do not wait for a rainy day to fix
your roof

The deed will praise itself

Anger is a brief madness, but it can
do damage that lasts forever

Respect tradition

You cannot lose what you never had

The pencil always lasts longer than
the eraser

Read carefully; sign cautiously

Do it better the second time around

Praise yourself

Experience creates knowledge

Your money is not your life

He who forgives ends the quarrel

When you compare your griefs with other people's, they will seem fewer

Never put off saying "I love you"

Live up to your reputation

Appetite rises to meet food supply

Other people's problems are more easily solved than your own

Nonviolence is a weapon of the strong

If you want to get more of something, then give more of that thing

The purpose of life is a life of purpose

Know when it is time to leave

A good short life is better than a long bad life

Look both ways before crossing

Conduct yourself with dignity

Hold yourself to a higher standard

To know how to do something well is
to enjoy it

Most discoveries are by error

It takes more than years to reach
maturity

Love your children for who they are,
not for what you want them to be

Every path leads two ways

Keep your eyes on the stars and
your feet on the ground
(Theodore Roosevelt)

Take all the help you can get

Be ashamed to catch yourself idle

Understand what you really have to
do in order to survive

We are by nature observers, and
thereby learners

Ride big waves

Inspiring wisdom can change your
life forever

It is easy to be wise after the fact

The arrow that leaves the bow
cannot come back

A boring life should be feared more
than death

Do not burn your bridge before you

No one has the power to write the
rules of love

Never tell tales out of school

Don't waste yourself in reflection

Jealousy and anger shorten life

One line of wisdom can change your
life more than volumes of books

The anticipation of a trip is often
more fun than the actual trip

Old age can be a great period
of calmness

Let yourself enjoy life

Many troubles are avoided by
leading a simple life

Simplify

A jackass can kick a barn
door down, but it takes
a carpenter to build one

Children make the best music

Pay attention

Prove them wrong

Seek out the opportunity in situations

The barrel is as strong as its hoops

Think positively and good things will happen

Cope with what life throws you

Do not get in the way of who you are

Never promise more than you are willing to give

Make people feel welcome by having flowers leading to your house

Love life

A smell can change your mood

Stop thinking about things that worry you

Least said, soonest mended

Be a good neighbor

Hatred can destroy a person's soul

Enjoy the things that go great together . . . like cookies and milk, peanut butter and jelly, pizza and beer

Adversity is a great teacher

Let your creative work be your inner playmate

Being tired is just a state of mind

Parents matter

Learn to unlearn

By asking questions you encourage other people to open up and let you in on their excitement about life

React with class

Don't try to fine-tune somebody else's view

Kindness is loving people more than they deserve

Winning or losing doesn't matter—it's how you play the game

Worry and dread are a waste of time

Good books are worth more than they cost

It takes a lot of courage to stick up for something you believe in

Work harder than the opposition

Never underestimate the power of
   a woman

A person can do himself more harm
   than others can do him

Don't pick your scabs

Setting the wheels in motion is
   a great first step

Hit your stride

Every honest job is dignified

Don't try to force people to live as
   you do

Good health and good sense are two
   of life's greatest blessings

Adversity tests whether you are
   what you thought your were

Wonder begins everything new

Honest labor needs no master

We find what we look for in
   this world

Heroes became heroes, flaws and all

To delay may mean to forget

Do it big or stay in bed

Know your children's friends

Time is more precious than things

Every man should be the intellectual proprietor of himself

It is better for happiness to find you than always to be searching for it

It is never too late to give up our prejudices

Think for yourself

Sit up straight

It takes two to communicate the truth—one to speak and another to hear (Henry David Thoreau)

We are all part of a large world

Dirt is not dirt, only matter in the wrong place

Every person has a unique past, present, and future

Motives are behind everything we do

It is more difficult to think than it is to react

Something big can be happening to more than one person at a time

When delegating, give away the power along with the job

Keep asking the right questions

Read for inspiration

The quest for wisdom ensures survival

The thinnest line is between love and hate

Do not let minor stress overwhelm you

Make something your specialty

Experience the bravery of people who struggle for mere survival

Dress for the job you want to have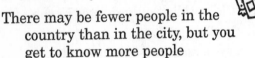

There may be fewer people in the country than in the city, but you get to know more people

Live while you are alive

A good leader is also a good follower

It takes more than strength to lead

The gaining of power changes every person

Good friendships are equal

Keep your eyes on the road

Out of the blue, send a love note to someone

Dare to reach out to someone you haven't met

Write down your work accomplishments

Begin a program of self-mastery

Carry a can-do attitude with you

Experience is what you get when looking for something else

Hear all and say nothing

Do not believe everything you hear

Do not take enjoyment from other people's pain

Be careful not to jump from the frying pan into the fire

Keep your nose clean

Always be a little kinder than necessary

Character takes a lifetime to develop

Do not gossip

Enjoy the journey as much as the stay

Learning from others' experiences is
easier than learning from your
own

Give a grateful man more than
he asks

Love has as many definitions as
there are people in love

A good friendship makes both people
better people

Hard work is the best investment
a man can make

You learn more on your own than
from other people

The quality of our lives depends,
to a large degree, on the results
of our decisions

Proceed as if you're not afraid

Always keep your word

Genius needs to be cultivated

Strive for excellence

Most of the things you worry about
never happen

Double-check your work

Wisdom is knowing what to overlook

Go with your gut feelings

It just takes one decision to change your life forever

Look for the favorable parts

Plan ahead nightly for the next day's work

Fight fair

Seek the positive elements and build on them

You cannot express thanks too often

Do not work just for the money

You can make your dreams come true if you wake up and work

Rank has its privileges

Read between the lines

Don't overschedule

Be inquisitive, ask many questions

Sit quietly and happiness may alight upon you

The greatest tragedy is indifference

Work while you wait

Life is meant to be lived with thought

Relish the details

Life will always improve

Be willing to commit yourself to
a course, perhaps a long and
hard one

Praise others for a job well done

Everybody thinks differently

Love yourself first and most

Skill and confidence are an
unconquerable army
(George Herbert)

Believe in the human race

Barking dogs seldom bite

If there is life, then there is hope

When you love someone, you need
to love both the good and bad

Be happy

We cannot do everything at once,
but we can do something at once
(Calvin Coolidge)

Give people more than they expect—
cheerfully

A person must make his opportunity
as often as he finds it

All fiction is based on fact

Having what you want and wanting
what you have are the same
thing

There is a difference between news
and gossip

The best way to make something last
is often to believe that it won't

Act constructively

Love is blind

Look through your heart concerning
matters of love

Let positive energy flow
through you

Kisses are meant to be returned

Something not understood can still
be useful

Your mind makes life exciting or dull

Banish the word *cannot* from your
vocabulary

Bad moods arrive unannounced

Life is relative to the circumstances
that surround you

Don't expect different results from
the same behavior

Doing the right thing is often painful

People who stay in the middle of the
road get run over

Find inspiration in others

Stop the busywork

Think before you commit to
something

Industry keeps the body healthy,
the mind clear, the heart whole,
the purse full

The ultimate measure of a man is
where he stands at times of
challenge and controversy

Telling the truth is a brave act

Understand why you do certain
things

Work with what you have

To each his own

Have passion for what you are doing

When you follow your heart, life becomes joyful

Time becomes more precious when there is less of it

Get rid of all the extras

Feel sorrow, but don't sink under its oppression

Follow your heart's desire and it will lead you to great adventures

Nothing is permanent except change

Children learn more when learning is fun

The bizarre can appear cool if it is in fashion

Do not go through life without leaving some kind of positive mark

Eat your honey, but stop when you're full

Never deprive someone of hope

Keep your fingers crossed

Learn an art where you cultivate beauty

Everything has two sides

Enjoy your successes while you
    are alive

The best charity is justice to all

Open yourself up to life's infinite
    possibilities

Do not be afraid of opposition

Love the unknown

A wise life is worth living

Everything comes to him who
    hustles while he waits
    (Thomas Alva Edison)

There is a key for every lock

Reading a great book can be
    a creative experience

Make simple a way of life

Life is filled with sacrifices

He who sows barley cannot gather
    wheat

Be strong, but never brutal

There is always more to know about
    everything

Your imagination needs exercise and
    nourishment

Noble gestures are as difficult as
they are rare

Happiness comes to those who are
self-sufficient

Life is a balancing act

If you are upset and feel like venting
your frustration, pour it out
on paper

Love should be guilt-free

Refrain from envy

Child rearing requires you to be
willing to bend

Don't throw away the old bucket
until you're sure the new one
holds water

Debt is a hard taskmaster

If you want to catch trout, don't fish
in a herring barrel

A coming misfortune must be borne
with patience

Learn from other people's mistakes

Forever is a long time

Do not hang all your clothes on
one nail

Pack light

It takes a lot of loving to make
a home

Tackle fears one at a time

Feet were made before wheels

Love adds purpose to life

More die of overfeeding than
underfeeding

Timing is everything

You always help yourself by helping
others

Keep your eyes wide open before
marriage, half shut afterward

Even getting older takes some
practice

We are surrounded by others; we can
choose to enjoy them or not

You do not always have to leave
home to take a vacation

Better to have an end to misery
than misery without end

Try to waste as little of life as
you can before you figure out
what is really important

Readiness is all

Be open to experience new people

A wise thing can be said in many
different ways

Be willing to shed parts of your
previous life

Nature can teach us much wisdom

A wise person knows when a
shortcut is actually a shortcut

Only by risking going too far can you
find out how far you can go

Greatness is in the heart

Let people know what you stand for
and what you will not stand for

Find out what you do best and stick
with it

When you're angry, take a thirty-
minute walk

A day in the country adds a day to
your life

The best judge of an argument
is time

Count your blessings

Anyone can be the subject of gossip

Approach life as if it were a banquet

Do not humiliate or ridicule a person in order to persuade him to change

Be aware of what you are worried about and why

You do not know how love will affect you before you fall in love

Dependence on another is perpetual disappointment

A fault denied is twice committed

Every person is born with a talent

Setting a good example is the best tool a parent can have in raising children

History can be as ambiguous as the future

If you hurry all the time, you hurry past all the good things in life

Learn not to try too hard

Good people can do bad things

A good idea is usually risky

Learning keeps a person young

Be punctual

Dreams can be valuable

Wisdom can come in the form of
a sudden revelation

Take charge of your own destiny

Most people do not know what
they are missing in life until
it is too late

Find meaning in leisure

Even the happiest people have
down days

Appreciate the questions as much as
the answers

Do not do anything just to say you
did it

Feel free to change your mind

The best successes come after
disappointments

Love is the way to capture meaning
in life

Sometimes not getting what you
want is a stroke of good luck

Your inner self needs external
    nourishment

It's easier to remember the name of
    someone who has power than
    that of someone who does not

Conceit is the most incurable disease
    known to the human soul

Reveal your inner beauty

Truly believing in yourself is a skill

Even during tough times remember
    to be a nice person

Purge unneeded information

If you do not take advantage of
    an opportunity, then someone
    else will

Replying well in conversation is just
    as important as listening well

Appreciate yourself

Love your neighbor

Smile when in doubt

Imagination rules the world

Always do the groundwork

The work is more important than
the glory

People condemn what they do not
understand

Never underestimate your power
to change yourself

Do what you would rather be doing

Use your life to make something that
will outlast it

Alter self-defeating patterns

Be tired of feeling tired

Too many pains take away from too
many pleasures

Celebrate being alive

The future changes everyone

Like a child plays, a genius works

Stop and think

Busy people do not have the time
to feel old

Advertise truthfully

Never give up your right to be wrong

Grass feels better to bare feet

Define for yourself what success is

Help yourself

Distrust interested advice (Aesop)

You are as happy as you decide to be

Tolerate ambiguity

We outgrow most things before they
are worn out

Hold your vision of peace clearly in
mind each day

You can never guard against chance

Take responsibility for your life

A good feeling gets better when it
is shared

Never tire of life

He who slings mud loses ground

Everybody's business is nobody's
business

Do your job and demand your
compensation—but in that order

If you are worrying about dying,
then you are not spending
enough time living

If it was easy to be successful, then
everyone would be

Deal with many of life's biggest problems with laughter

Keep a daily log of the wonders you experience

Gardening is great exercise

When you say no, mean no

Good or bad, most things do not last long

There are five enemies of peace: avarice, ambition, envy, anger, and pride (Ralph Waldo Emerson)

Create from what you know

Do your Christmas shopping early

The end of something is actually a new beginning in disguise

Play should never be work

Innocence can only be taken away once

Charity begins at home

Think in clear thoughts

Haste makes waste

A person's worth cannot be measured by a test

Tell a good employee how much she is appreciated

Success can bring envy

A lie can never fix the truth

Live out loud

The better you do, the lower the profile you should keep

When opportunity knocks, open the door

Walk the opposite direction from imitation

All that shines is not gold

Aim high

It is better to embrace a moment than it is to fear the moment passing

Sometimes being alone is the best medicine

Listen attentively

No one can talk for more than five minutes without exposing the extent of his ignorance

Do not delay acting on a good idea

Friendship is a big part of one's life

Life means what you want it to

There is always a light at the end
of the tunnel

Enjoy yourself

Think why you are saying no before
you say no

Optimism is a great healing force

Life is short

Mind unemployed is mind unenjoyed

Virtue is the fruit of life

Own each day

Show up for life

Patronize local merchants

Education makes darkness light

It ain't over till it's over (Yogi Berra)

Children act in the village as they
have learned at home

Keep your sense of wonder

It takes one to know one

Fair is fair

We do not have to be perfect to live
a spiritual life

The pores of the mind should be left
open to all impressions

Listen much and speak little

If you do not claim too much
intelligence, people will give you
credit for more than you have

Influence begins with the parents
and ends with the peers

The things which hurt, instruct
(Benjamin Franklin)

Accentuate the positive

Be a poor hater

Little things can mean a lot

To be without some of the things you
want is an indispensable part of
happiness (Bertrand Russell)

Nothing is as easy as it looks

If nothing went wrong, life would be
pretty boring

Many words can describe a simple
thing

Everything we do tells something about us

Actions speak louder than words

Face the realities of death and calamity; look at painful events squarely

When you are down, surround yourself with friends who are up

Look other people in the eye

He climbs highest who helps another up

Smile

The secret to staying younger is living honestly, eating slowly, and just not thinking about your age (Lucille Ball)

You have to pay a price for life's rewards

The life which is unexamined is not worth living (Plato)

Everyone has a gift for something

Natural abilities need pruning like natural plants

Being alive is its own reward

Put your house in order

It takes great strength to be happy

Do not press luck too far

Great things are accomplished
with passion

Careless hurry may cause endless
regret

People's best traits cannot be
measured tangibly

Health and happiness usually
go together

Love begins in the eyes, then quickly
goes to the heart, and only
sometimes ends up in the brain

A roving eye misses opportunities
close by

Don't bring up old wounds

Stay faithful to yourself

Face the music

Take the road less traveled

Be friendly and you will
never want for friends

There is no formula for living
a happy life

Take risks

Wisdom is acquired when you want
it to be

There is no foreign language for
laughter

It is difficult to be happy when
things are not going right,
but not impossible

Remember that relationships
take time

Age can teach contentment

Do the day's work

You can have anything you want
but you can't have everything
you want

No matter where the body is,
the mind can still be free

It is part of the cure to wish to
be cured

Before you make a fuss, ask yourself
first: is it worth it?

Be kind in all you do and say

What are you waiting for?

Faith is daring the soul to go beyond
what the eyes can see

If you can sell it to yourself, then you
can sell it to anyone

A great dessert can wipe away the
memory of a bad meal

If you can't say anything nice, don't
say anything at all

It takes incredible strength to give

Retiring means enjoying a second
childhood

Treat your friends like family and
your family like friends

Long-lasting lessons are usually
learned at a steep price

Love is a great investment

Nothing succeeds like persistence

There is little assurance when we
entrust our happiness to others

Be moderate in all things

Some things look better from
a distance

Look for the truth

Take your hobbies seriously

Knowledge frees a person

Knowledge is gained by hard work
and desire

Do not expect kids to listen to your
advice and ignore your examples

Let your character speak for you

Be kind to strangers

In between birth and death, you can
do a lot of living

Don't try to explain everything

The only person who never, ever
forgets your birthday is you

Seek honor first, pleasure will follow

Obstacles are meant to be
surmounted

Appreciate being happy

Spend your time and energy creating
not criticizing

Completion is a habit

Your conversation is the mirror of
your thoughts

It's not the goal but the set of the
   sail that determines the way
   you go

Mind over matter

Be good and you'll be happy

You never know a person until you
   live with her

Accept what comes and meet it with
   courage

Sometimes it is better to incur a loss
   than to make a gain

The past was once the future

Freedom is one of the easiest things
   to abuse

Keep facing toward change

Become a skilled learner

Learn with enthusiasm

Wish for your happiness more than
   the unhappiness of others

Everything is easy if you enjoy
   doing it

Recognize the difference between the
   great and small things in life

It is not who is right but what is right that's important

Silence is often the key to success

Every minute you are angry you lose sixty seconds of happiness

You get what you pay for

Hesitate for a good reason

Learn to seek satisfaction in a job well done

Never depend on the admiration of others

Laughing at your own jokes makes them funny to at least one person

There is no harm in asking

When you realize you've made a mistake, try to correct it

Freedom is within everyone's grasp

When you inspire others, you are truly rich

When love and skill work together, expect a masterpiece

Practice what you preach

One should not be in a hurry to
be distressed

Bury "can't" and you'll find "will"

Do not look for wrong and evil

Trust yourself

Everything sounds romantic in
a foreign language

Choose work that is in harmony with
your values

Grandparents treat their
grandchildren differently from
the way they treated their
children

The less you have, the more content
you can be

No man is an island

Set a good example

Decide on an inner discipline to
protect yourself

Give thanks for your food

Successful leaders inspire other
people

We are all citizens of the world

Eat what you like

Ninety percent of life involves drudgery, so make the other 10 percent count

Know when to forgive yourself

The unknown is feared by weak souls

Profit from your mistakes

The conditions will never be perfect

Never send a dog to deliver a steak

Be open to new ideas

It is okay to be content with what you have, but not with what you are

Greed creates waste

Work your mind and body together

Nature's laws are constantly changing

Luck favors those who are prepared

The end of desire brings peace

Self-confidence is the best confidence

Reinvent yourself

Prayer is a wish turned upward

Girls will be girls

Desire for your neighbor what you
desire for yourself

Get your heart to be conciliatory

Life cannot repeat itself

We're all eligible for life's small
pleasures

Life is not sold with a guarantee

The door to success is always
marked "push"

Sacrifice is a key to enjoyment

When the going gets tough,
the tough get going

Encouragement from a good teacher
can turn a student's life around

The best is yet to be

When talking to people smarter
than you, something is bound
to rub off

Make a wish list

Living a good life should be
exhausting

Doing is more valuable than saying

Action without thought is like
shooting without aim

Gaining someone's trust is
an awesome feeling

With the power of thought comes
the ability to think positively
or negatively

Never talk to a drunken or
angry man

It is better to make an enemy
than an excuse

Knowledge grows like a tree:
slowly and on fertile ground

Children and war do not mix

Use delicate politeness in
your friendships

Knowing how to find knowledge is
the first step toward wisdom

Ask for a raise when you have
earned it

You never get the past back

Nature works 24 hours a day, 7 days
a week, 365 days a year

Some questions have no answers

Recognize opportunities

Try to make someone happy each
and every day

Once you find you are interested in
a subject, dive in

Become better than you were

Make sure your dreams help you

Actions and words are the windows
through which the heart is seen

Be a good friend

Pride yourself on virtue

You do not have to keep running
after you have caught the bus

In a good relationship, each person
helps the other one grow

Money often costs too much

Take the credit where it is due

Keep your head when those around
you are losing theirs

Whatever interests, is interesting

Always keep your spurs on

If you fail to plan, you are planning
to fail

A life should not be judged until
it is over

Truths last forever

Be willing to change the way you
play the game

Acknowledge a gift, no matter how
small

Adversity is like taxes and death;
it happens to everyone

What the eyes see can change what
the mind believes

Education is a great equalizer

Adventures are enjoyed even more
when you get home

Once a decision is reached,
stop worrying

Hate seldom disappears on its own

Be as useful as you can

A career never takes the place of
a home where love reigns

You cannot undo anything that you
did in the past

Art can free the soul

Change happens to most people
    unconsciously

Sometimes you need other people in
    order to reach an individual goal

Pain nourishes courage

People like people who
    complement/compliment them

Remorse is the poison of life

Ambitious people are never bored

Sometimes old methods of dealing
    with things do not work

Take everything in stride

Never be idle

Do not get off the ladder before you
    reach the ground

Darkness teaches you to appreciate
    light

Your children can embarrass you
    better than anyone

Use a good mind well

In unity there is strength

Courtesy costs nothing and is
    contagious

Limits must be tested

Anxiety brings old age too soon

The fear of change is usually far worse than the actual change

Success always requires a certain amount of order

The more things change, the more they are the same (Alphonse Karr)

Invest heavily in yourself

A disease known is half cured

Leave much to show for the time you spend here

A true smile occurs when the mouth and heart are coordinated

Advice is what we ask for when we already know the answer but wish we didn't

Communicate your ideals by example

Believe in hope, work, family, learning, knowing, loving, and with a little luck, happiness will come

To act is easy; to understand is hard

Let yourself be capable of showing emotions

Everyone meets the future

What lies behind and before us are small matters compared to what lies within us

A kind heart is a fountain of gladness

Leave your mark on life while you have it in your power

The more people become educated, the more they become equal

Public office is a public trust

You always find time to do the things you really want to do

Fools rush in where angels fear to tread

Keep questioning

Don't judge people by appearances

Some ideas will last forever

Understand your strengths and weaknesses

Trust in your own untried capacity

Don't go to bed angry

Learn to complete what you begin

Do what you love and success
will follow

If you fear death, then you cannot
live

When love beckons, follow it

Poetry is more than just written
words

Make sure you are understood

Treat humanity as a means as well
as an end

Do it right the first time

Traveling up a hill is easier on
a bicycle built for two than
on a bicycle built for one

Keep breathing

Play has a high value

Believe in other people's potential

Let happy thoughts heal the soul

No one is better than anyone else

Focus on the big picture

Ask questions instead of issuing orders

Fear either makes you strive to accomplish things or stops you

Everybody is ignorant, only on different subjects (Will Rogers)

Things have a way of happening that need to happen

If you have to whisper it, better not say it

If you dare to fail miserably, you can achieve greatly

There is no one universal definition of a family

Everyone to his own opinions

Wealth is a state of mind

Your achievements live longer than you

Music hath charms to soothe the savage beast

Peace of mind is always present; you just have to learn how to find it

You need the will to succeed in order to succeed

The eraser disappears before
the pencil

Love is the cornerstone,
the foundation

Everyone can have a happy life,
but not everyone wants to

Some people have to be burned
before they learn

Joy is the best wine

Keep your foot on the mark

The paradox of life: when you are
young, you want to be older;
when you are old, you want
to be younger

Build castles in the air, but put
foundations under them

It is better to live with gusto than
watch life pass you by

The ladder is ascended step by step

You must shift your sail with
the wind

There is no perfect pleasure unless
the conscience is at rest

Action is our chief joy

Every joy has its sorrow

If you think about tomorrow,
    then you are not living today

Everything belongs to nature

Listen and learn

Read every day

Life is art, not science

Everyone can become intimidated

You will experience everything if you
    live long enough

Resist the desire to tell people how
    they can do something better

Envy is the biggest cause of ruined
    friendships

Spend more energy on the things
    that make you happy and less
    energy on the things that make
    you unhappy

Love is the heart's power

The only food for thought is
    more thought

Act like the person you want to be

Some people who enter our lives
change it forever

Kind words can be short and easy
to speak

Suffering can make you stronger

Unless you can do better, do not
criticize

The memory that you leave behind
is your memorial

The future is never sure

The optimist makes his own
heaven and enjoys it as he
goes through life

Never underestimate the power
of love

Angry thoughts make angry people

A diamond is a chunk of coal made
good under pressure

Manage stress

Life's "withs" and "withouts"
are about equal

One fantasy can transform one
million realities

You cannot experience happiness
    unless you can forgive yourself

The bonds of matrimony are like
    financial bonds: if the interest
    is not kept up, they become
    worthless

It pays to be on the level

Don't make a date for anything more
    than a month in advance

Even if you do not see something,
    you can still have faith that
    it is there

Even givers have their limits

Everyone is beautiful with a smile

No great person ever complains of
    want of opportunity

He that has knowledge spares his
    words

Find out what you like doing best
    and get someone to pay you for
    doing it

Compare yourself to you

Enter a room with nothing to prove

String your pearls on a strong cord

Add up the experiences of your life to total a great sum

An insult lasts longer than an injury

Some things seem easy at first, but they are easier said than done

Nobody dies of a broken heart

The world likes a happy person

Love comes unseen

Do not try to seem wise to others

We are living examples

Muddy water, if permitted to remain still, will gradually become clear

Don't save anything good for later

Concentrate on everything you do

Children respect parents who respect them

Doubt is the key to knowledge

Face adversity with a smile

A fault confessed is half redressed

If you are wrong, at least be wrong with style

Hang in there

Courage is not the absence of fear
   but the ability to carry on with
   dignity in spite of it (Scott Turow)

There is more room outside than
   inside

You are older longer than you
   are younger

Will this be important five years
   from now?

Mistakes are all there waiting
   to be made

Each person can contribute
   something special in life

Spiritual travel has many routes

Suppressing a moment of anger may
   save a day of sorrow

Don't try to change what can't be
   changed

He who anticipates good fortune
   risks it by his presumption

Everyone is ignorant of some things;
   but try not to be ignorant
   of yourself

Return all phone calls

If you give someone an inch,
   they will take a mile

Time is money

The public loves someone who smiles

Treat yourself to occasional luxuries

Stay on your toes

Your reason and passion are the
   rudder and sails of your soul

If you would be a writer, write

Enjoy what you can

Rise above little things

Encourage anyone trying to improve

Nothing succeeds like success

With more knowledge comes
   greater doubt

Ask your heart what actions to take

Accept that life on life's terms may
   not always be to our liking or
   to our understanding

Learn to live by the motto
   "Do it now"

It is natural to want to feel free

To be able to act on something is
one skill; to be able to act on
something quickly is an entirely
different skill

One person's leisure is another
person's work

By explaining a joke, it loses
its humor

Be content with what you have

A liar is not believed when he speaks
the truth

Make your career fit your personality

What you do not like as a follower,
do not do as a leader

Quietly accept events as they occur

A genius simplifies the complex

Poetry is like philosophy

Everything is good for something

Freedom is taken for granted by
the free

The key to freedom is in your mind

Lying damages the present as well as
the future

Buy low, sell high

Diversify your investments

Decency and inner beauty are more
valuable than appearance

Allow for human nature

Be willing to learn from friends
and family

Teaching is easier than learning

Less can be more

The generous man receives more
than he gives

Push your luck sometimes

A simple life is not that expensive

Cut in half the number of things
you have to do each day

Great people do great things

You can't know everything

A smart student can always
overcome poor teaching

There are no advantages to
resentment

Write down your goals

You cannot live down a lie

You're nothing if you're not excited
by what you're doing

Use encouragement; make the fault
seem easy to correct

Educate the heart

Drink at least eight glasses of water
a day

You cannot cheat against yourself

No one is born hating

Every journey has its share of
setbacks and failures

Stop asking people for things they
cannot give you

A leopard cannot change its spots

Your opinions are within your control

Living life on life's terms combines
moments of happiness with
moments of sadness

A good life keeps away wrinkles

Understand the value of things

A person's laugh is as unique as
his fingerprints

Do not misuse your strengths

Get mad for the right reasons

Intuition can help you determine
if something bothers someone

Confidence begets confidence

Love for the joy of loving

People respond to chutzpah

The art of being a good guest is
knowing when to leave

The mind can make things better
or worse than they actually are

A garden looks more beautiful from
a little distance than up close

Helping other people with their
troubles helps you forget your
own

Dreams can become real

Conciliate those you cannot conquer

Open up

We can find great comfort in the
experiences of those traveling
the path with us

Wisdom can be achieved through
observation

Creative mess is preferable to idle neatness

A parent's disapproval is a powerful force

Perform more than promised rather than promise more than perform

Do not end up where you do not think you belong

You are made up from a combination of your genes and your environment

It is easy to hold the fort when it is not attacked

Take time in turning a corner

When people talk about the weather, the conversation cannot last longer than five minutes

Resisting change has a steep price

A thought precedes every action

What is well planted cannot be uprooted

Beggars should not be choosers

Time is more valuable to the elderly than to the young

Life is what you make it

Perfection is impossible

Become the moment

Read to your children every night

Keep an open mind

Do not make everything in life work

Look at the source as well as
the advice

Youth is the most precious resource
on earth

Seek quality

Anticipation of pleasure and pain is
always greater than the reality
of it

The purpose of criticism is to help

They are weak who declare fate
the sole cause

He who plants kindness gathers love

Big life-altering changes need
small starts

Be committed

Be that which you would make
others

Leisure is at its best when one is so
busy that a little leisure time is
the goal

An ounce of prevention is worth
a pound of cure

It is better to try to change yourself
than to try to change mankind

Character is what we are; reputation
is what others think we are

Like seeks like

A person who does kind acts is not
always a kind person

Once you say something it is out
of your control

Name the situation as it is

Fear is a great inventor

Pleasing yourself is usually more
difficult than pleasing others

You do not need to convince others
that you are clever, sophisticated,
affable

The more things you plan to do, the
more energy you will have

Spend your years ripening instead
of rotting

You are largely what you think
you are

Don't procrastinate

The more we want, the less we have

The best of the journey is getting
home

People forget the failures of others
very quickly

Nothing ventured, nothing gained

Time lasts the same amount whether
you are feeling fine or poorly

Anything worth having is worth
working for

Any mistake is food for a new
invention

Know where you stand at all times

Listen to music that comforts you

Take pains or the pains will take you

Maintain hope

Don't burn your bridges
behind you

Change is a challenge for the
courageous, an opportunity
for the alert

Your ability to change, changes
the world

In order to learn, we must pay
attention

Be grateful that God doesn't answer
all your prayers

Contentment is worth more than
riches

Laughing at yourself can cure
many things

We do not stay young for a reason

Retirement can be a lot more than
just a permanent vacation

Show respect for all living things

Select the illusion that appeals to
your temperament and embrace
it with passion to be happy

Passion leads to success

Time is a state of mind

Help when needed is the best kind
of help

Sometimes help comes from the
strangest source

Apologize liberally

You profit from praise if you value
criticism

Never do evil hoping that good will
come of it

If you want something changed,
gather support and change it

Perform your job better than anyone
else can

View reality from a distance

Organize your day in the morning

Time teaches us all things

Never leave home without a sense
of humor

Humor is to life what shock
absorbers are to automobiles

Sometimes it takes a long time
to get someplace

A good cry can be very therapeutic

Laughter helps you recover more
quickly

Don't be afraid to say no

Do nice things for others without telling anyone about it

If you remember the bad also take time to remember the good

Do not be deceived by flattery

Be conscious when you attain freedom

Not everything can be defined

We should be glad we do not get everything we ask for

There are three types of people: those with wishbones, those with funny bones, and those with backbones

The best way to succeed is to do small things well

Singing is good for your soul

By thinking of ourselves less, we learn to love ourselves more

When in doubt, abstain

Big things of the world can only be achieved by attending to small details

Friendships take work

Do nothing by halves

Difficult and painful times should
make you better, not bitter

There is no one way to believe in God

Love will find a way

He who is all for himself is often all
by himself

Have a nice day

A river begins with one drop of water

A warning is enough for wise people

Delays increase desires or
extinguish them

You make someone feel good when
you use one of her suggestions

How old would you be if you did not
know your age?

You cannot do a kindness too soon

Your mind controls whether you live
in a paradise or hell

Education is a gift that none can
take away

Eat smaller portions

Dealing with someone who is angry
    is easier than dealing with
    someone who is silent

Rebuild broken relationships

Want to succeed

There is nothing wrong in admitting
    your are afraid

Remember to live

Wake up!

Charity should be the rule not
    the exception

Do not lose the substance by
    grasping at the shadow

Ability helps you get to the top, but
    character keeps you from falling

Speaking softly can usually gain
    more attention than shouting

Practice living life by your own rules

Seize every opportunity to give
    encouragement

Stop disappointing yourself

Discipline with a gentle hand

Fortune does not lie at the end of the rainbow; it is found behind some obstacles

You must be alive in order to live life

Learn how to prepare at least five meals expertly

Excellence is possible without perfection

You do not need to justify asking questions

Understand each age's limit

An imagination is a terrible thing to waste

See everything as though for the first time

Mistakes are opportunities to learn

Love makes everyone vulnerable

No man is above the law

If you want to grow, look at things differently

Forcing yourself to be active is the hardest part of being active

Hope exists in everyone

Do not meddle with business you
    know nothing about

Alter your life by altering your
    attitudes

Do not read magazines with more
    ads than content

Let others know where you stand

Truth is shorter than fiction

Knowledge needs to be acquired
    to be had

Whenever you are true to yourself,
    you will be true to others

Apply the wisdom attained from
    the books you read

Do your own thing

An hour in the morning is worth two
    in the evening

A little spark kindles a great fire

Imitate the successes of the wise and
    not the mistakes of the fools

Ambition knows no moderation

When the cat's away, the mice
    will play

Keep your ears open

Talking about your problems does not always help

Life begins when you start to understand

A good listener is popular everywhere, and after a while he knows something

Humankind is just a small part of nature

What sunshine is to flowers, smiles are to humanity

A beautiful soul lasts longer than a beautiful body

Real life should never be totally replaced by a virtual one

Guilty is its own punishment

Be adaptable

One teacher can change the world

Be guided by your dreams

Successful people learn to use patience

Treat others just as you love to be treated yourself

Help never comes too late

In the end, things will mend

Second childhoods come with age

Don't overanalyze

Don't overreact

There are as many characters as there are individuals

Sometimes you need a little push to get back on track

A clean conscience is a good pillow

Education brings people to different places

Getting fired can be a blessing

Cool your temper

Give a little, take a little

Express yourself artistically

You cannot play in dirt without getting dirty

Experience is a hard teacher

A sure way to fail is to be overconfident

Nobody enjoys the company of a braggart

You can always hope

Make new friends but keep
the old ones

Give up on the idea that more
is better

Do not let words get in the way
of action

Assuage distress with a smile

Know a horse by riding him;
a person by associating with him

Find more ways to find joy in
everyday life

One wish enjoyed at a time is more
satisfying than many granted
at once

Old age does not have to curb
enthusiasm

Neither be all nor give all to anyone

You are what you eat

Treat people as if they were what
they should be

What is quickly done is quickly
undone

Make your house a home

Always keep a pad and pencil nearby
    so you can write down ideas,
    solutions, and thoughts as
    they occur

Be graceful when you're feeling bad

Life is a song to sing

Know when you know the truth

Practice makes perfect

Remember to say please

Ignorance is the root of misfortune

People will take you much at your
    own reckoning

Listen to the true geniuses of
    the world

You are what you do

Live your life doing good for the sake
    of doing good

A day lost is never found

Power tends to always want
    more power

Love is a chemical reaction

Free yourself from a trapped life

The customer is always right

We cannot decide what may happen
to us, but we can decide what
happens in us

An idea cannot be jailed

There is no substitute for hard work
(Thomas Alva Edison)

Begin nothing until you have
considered how it is to be finished

Be charitable in your speech, actions,
and judgment

Do the right thing

Nothing is said that has not been
said before

Make something significant of your
existence

Develop and maintain a capacity
to forgive

Intentions as well as actions must be
good to be acceptable

Even an old body can have a young
mind

Happiness should be a part of love

What is impossible to change is best
to forget

Knowledge needs a strong
   foundation on which to grow

He who hates is lost

Defy time

Whine less, breathe more

Keep your wonder of great and
   noble things

Laughter is a universal sound

Ideas never work unless you do

You can discover new things in life
   every day

The more we can enjoy ourselves
   and others, the more we can
   accomplish, help, and create

Regardless of age, we all need about
   the same amount of love

See yourself as successful

Do not go near the water unless
   you know how to swim

Love can make everything look
   clearer

Only your mind can make things
   impossible

Forgiving someone is a sign
of strength

Seeing is believing

Spend more time with friends than
with enemies

When you get together with friends,
do more than just get together

He is prudent who is patient

It is easier to be rich than to
be beautiful

Every tale can be told in
a different way

Having common enemies makes for
a strong friendship

Take the bull by the horns

People's needs change

Lose a small fish to catch a big one

A calamity is often a blessing
in disguise

Find need in your existence

Chart your own course

Set aside quiet time every day

Practice ignoring your negative
thoughts

Balance centers you

Quality cannot be defined, but is
easily seen

Keep your word, even to your
enemies

Doing something you love is never
a waste of time

It is better to bend than to break

Mental wounds take longer to heal
than physical ones

Sometimes life feels like a terrible
struggle, but only sometimes

Grandparents are parents with
a second chance

There are many things we have to
figure out on our own

Every person's punishment or
reward is that he has to put up
with himself

Start at the beginning and work your
way through it

Embrace change

There are two sides to every story

You can tell a lot about a person by the way he walks

Age changes your opinions on all important aspects of life

The truth makes us free

Good judgment comes from experience and experience comes from bad judgment

The primary goal of education is to make people better people

Ignorance is no excuse

Exercise your mind

Laughter breaks up seriousness

In action you have the power to grow

Death cannot be reversed

Live according to spiritual principles

Be willing to lose a battle in order to win the war

Utilize what you have

Many great people were late bloomers

Don't intentionally embarrass
  someone

A day is only as long as you
  are awake

The way to tell a good wine is if you
  like it

It is more difficult to be beautiful
  than to be intelligent

It does not cost anything to be kind

Be open to new suggestions

Conversation is an art

Do not corner a rat

Great oaks grow from little acorns

Always have something beautiful
  in sight

Open your heart

Attitudes are more important
  than facts

Eat well-balanced meals

Don't tell others what is good

Be happy where you are

Live with the consciousness of a poet

Work never hurt anybody

Use humor to find your way into
people's hearts

There may be luck in getting a good
job, but there is no luck in
keeping it

If love is not allowed to grow, then it
will die

Actions make history

Paint masterpieces

Learning from history eliminates
many mistakes

We are usually stronger than we
think we are

Don't judge people, love them

Silence is the best defense for
ignorance

Know the people who know you

Don't criticize a gift

Cry if it makes you feel better

Be tough-minded but tenderhearted

Do the right thing, no matter what
others think

Desire nothing that would bring
   disgrace

Gaining knowledge is its own
   pleasure

See a world in a grain of sand
   and heaven in a wild flower
   (William Blake)

Avoid telling others your ambitions
   as they might try to discourage
   you

Avoid petty and useless things

A marriage is made in heaven,
   but the details are worked
   out on earth

By exploring your underlying beliefs,
   you gain a better picture of your
   life's goals

There is nothing either good or bad,
   but thinking makes it so
   (Shakespeare)

Happiness adds and multiplies as we
   divide it with others

Heroes take risks

Call people by name

Change in order to lead a better life

Live life with high expectations

Bloom more than once

Change your routines to revitalize
yourself

Feel the music as well as hear it

Control your passion or it will
control you

A mob has more heads than brains

Your best friend is yourself

Look for yourself

Do not speak unless you can improve
on silence

Nothing is simple anymore

It is more desirable to be thought
great by others than by yourself

The older you get, the more precious
life becomes

It is better to be careful than to
be sorry

Life is sometimes more than just
doing the best that you can

Realize life is a gift, not a right

Listening and speaking are two different skills

You can't buy friendship

Enjoy what you have instead of feeling sorry for what you do not have

Seize what is highest and you will possess what is in between

The most important words we say are those to ourselves about ourselves

Never outgrow fun

You can have a lot of friends and still feel lonely

Count to ten before you get angry

We are all treasure chests of talents, insights, and remarkable gifts

Knowledge begins as a foundation; blocks need to be added to it until you reach the top

Our own success should contribute to the success of others

Divide and conquer

Don't use your teeth to
open things

Give courage to the timid

Each new invention is eventually
replaced by a newer invention

Don't expect others to take as much
interest in you as you do yourself

Do not think only in absolutes

The easy stuff does not teach
us much

'Tis better to have loved and lost,
than never to have loved at all
(Alfred Lord Tennyson)

The student should always pass
the teacher

Try not to outlive your mind
and body

Panic can be used for energy

It is never too late to go back
to school

Get it in writing

Connect with your soul mates

The weaker the argument,
the stronger the words

Speaking good about someone behind his back gets back to him just as quickly as speaking badly

That which blossoms must also decay

Miracles multiply with sharing

Sanity often means that we do not act on our first impulse

There is no garden without weeds

Don't resist a generous impulse

Love is about acceptance

The troubles you make for yourself are harder to deal with than the troubles others make for you

Ignore the inconsequential

See everything; overlook a great deal; correct a little

A tongue's slip is a truth's revelation

One of the most frightening things in the world is someone with nothing to lose

To gain experience, one must live

A quiet child is plotting mischief, or has done it

Taking risks for a reason is different
from just taking risks

Assume responsibility for the quality
of your own life

Work hard and prepare yourself,
then your chance will come

All ambitious people experience
many failures

Every why has a wherefore

Mistakes are often the best teachers

Better to face danger than always to
be in fear

Gain strength from people who
love you

Never send a chicken to bring home
a fox

Don't look back, someone might be
gaining on you

Degrees of happiness are achieved
through perspective

Do not argue if you know you
are wrong

When the fruit is ripe, it falls

Love cannot be forced

Solution is possible where acceptance
is ready

Wearing the right clothes can hide
many physical flaws

Do not count your chickens before
they are hatched (Aesop)

We are judged by what we finish,
not on what we start

Love creates love

A little nonsense now and then is
relished by the best of men

Get in touch with your feelings

Enlightenment is the closest you can
come to living life as a child

Before you try to convince anyone
else, be sure you are convinced

Ya gotta do what ya gotta do

Decide exactly what you have
to achieve

Wisdom depends on personal
vigilance

Ask questions and learn

You remember giving longer than
you remember getting

Have patience with all things

In order to believe in something
you must first agree with it

People know a fool when they
meet one

When you come to the end of your
rope, tie a knot and hang on

Work hard

If you have done it right, being
an adult is more fun than
being a child

Make do without the things you
cannot get

No words ever spoken to you should
change the way you feel about
yourself

Spend less money than you have

Makeovers start from within

Don't be curious for no purpose

Power at the moment will probably
not be the power at the next
moment

Be enthusiastic about the success
of others

Your time will come

First deserve, then desire

Things can always get better

Great songs happen when music and
poetry agree

Keep good company and you will be
counted one of them

Have the faith to move mountains

The past can only be relived in the
mind, not undone

Compassion will cure more than
condemnation

Love can teach you to do many
things

Forgive your parents

Being patient cures many ills

Planning a vacation is sometimes as
much fun as experiencing it

In truth lies beauty

Always keep some of the past
with you

There is no future like the present

First catch your rabbit, then make
   your stew

Cut yourself some slack

Glory needs an audience to exist

Don't spend time wishing for things
   you don't have

Add a little happiness to your life
   each day

Love is for eternity

Move around a room with style

Be patient in steadily working
   toward your goals

Learn, see, do something beautiful
   every day as a prescription for
   happiness

Intelligent people err, too

Happiness is a form of courage

Tell people (today) how much you
   love them

Life's most treasured moments often
   come unannounced

In times of stress, visualize
   tranquility

If you can dream it, you can
    realize it

Drive your dreams

Know when to take a break

Be careful what you wish for

Education sets you free

You cannot make people care about
    something

Be friends with your family

Well begun is half done (Horace)

If you know where you are and what
    you have to do, then it is easier to
    figure out how to do it

Compliment others

Live in balance

Don't peek into a cannon

Smell the roses

The key to failure is trying to
    please everybody

Nothing is hard if you understand it

Respect the rules

Grief does not change a thing

Do not rely on your wits alone

There is a limit to everything

Often we hold friends by holding our tongues

Distance allows you to see things more clearly

Instead of loving your enemies, treat your friends a little better

Seek the best

Things are not always what they seem

Insight and knowledge produce enlightenment

He who knows what is enough will always have enough

You are judged not by what you have but by what you do with what you have

Develop your own rituals

Do not overwork a willing horse

Circumstances are the instruments of the wise

Do not let life dry you up before it is time

Be prepared for the unexpected

Make living itself an art

History is only as accurate as
the historian

People are designed to be able to do
almost anything

The gaining of knowledge is man's
greatest gift

The secret of success is doing
something you love

Keep the peace within yourself
and then you can bring peace
to others

One adventure will lead to another

You invite future injuries if you
revive past ones

Create in your spare time

You can't tell a book by its cover

Do not boast of a thing until it
is done

Your mind can be slowed down while
your body is still speeding

There is good and bad in everything

Each individual has the choice to make her own life either complicated or simple

A change of work is as good as a rest

Even Napoleon had his Watergate (Yogi Berra)

Life is a series of lessons that must be lived to be understood (Ralph Waldo Emerson)

As you grow older, your parents become smarter

Do not bite the hand that feeds you

Everyone gets the same twenty-four hours in a day—the difference is how you use it

Read between the lines

Make history

Learn every step of the way

You must do the thing you think you cannot do

Spoken words and lost opportunities can't be recalled

The best judge knows the least

Remember your duty

There are two sides to every story

Eat sparingly

Go home and love your family

The more you depend on someone else, the more you have to accommodate him

In difficult moments, visualize a favorite place

Forget a wrong, remember a kindness

Zero in on your target and go for it

Illusions can be more gratifying than reality

Better a good conscience without wisdom than wisdom without a good conscience

You do not always have to qualify playtime

Bite your tongue

A room without books is like a body without a soul (Cicero)

Dare yourself to love more

It costs more to avenge than to endure injuries

Honor shall uphold the humble
in spirit

Watch, listen, understand

Know where the exits are
located

Do not let people bring you down
to their level

People who fight fire with fire
usually end up with ashes

Much of life's information becomes
irrelevant after a week

Not everything can be put in order

Act as though it is impossible to fail
at a difficult task

Think for yourself and let others
enjoy the right to do the same

If you do not know something, know
where to find out about it

Bad weather can ruin the best-laid
designs

Opportunity sooner or later comes to
all who work and wish

A little knowledge is good, a lot
is better

Know how to wait for the right
 moment

An intelligent person is one
 who knows when to keep
 his mouth shut

Happiness comes from a person's
 character

Know if people want to hear what
 you want to say

Keep your desk neat

Flowers feed the soul

Better to remain silent and be
 thought a fool, than to speak
 out and remove all doubt
 (Abraham Lincoln)

Ideas build upon each other

It often shows a fine command of
 language to say nothing

Make choices out of love

Keep your broken arm inside
 your sleeve

If you do evil, expect to suffer evil

When something in your life breaks
 down, put it back together again

Hug away things that are
bothering you

Never help a child with a task at
which he feels he can succeed

Music is the least disagreeable of
all noises

You can do anything if you have
passion

Don't worry about what other people
are thinking of you

Don't talk about people behind
their backs

Having money does not mean you
are happy

Study hard

Reveal only what you have to

Effort achieves our wishes

It's all right letting yourself go, as
long as you can get yourself back

Turn knowledge into ideas

Understand that life is not fair

Leave your shoes at the front door

If you want to catch fish, you can't
mind getting wet

The world is different when you are
awake than when you are asleep

Intelligence is not enough; using
intelligence wisely is the key

Switch from autopilot to manual

Love who loves you

When life is finally figured out,
there is not enough time to
do everything you want

Never criticize someone until you've
walked a mile in his shoes

Spend some of your time protecting
the earth

A person's value is that which he sets
upon himself

The brightest sunshine produces
the darkest shadows

A flow will have an ebb

It is impossible to be happy and
envious at the same time

Idleness is the refuge of weak minds
and the holiday of fools

New things become used things
the next day

No one can serve two masters

Happiness can only be felt if you
don't set any condition

Keep helpful advice and get rid of
harmful advice

You may have the right to be angry,
but not the right to be cruel

Show enthusiasm even when you
don't feel like it

Make important decisions when you
are in a good mood

Too much leisure, like too much of
anything, is not healthy

No amount of money can cure
an unhappy mind

A nap a day keeps the doctor away

Each man has his own vocation,
the talent is the call

Make sure your faults are not
dangerous to you or others

Watching encourages a meditative
state

Avoid the redundant

Keep busy

Don't fret about winning awards

Each new generation thinks that it is
the one inventing life

Loose lips sink ships

Children are better observers than
adults

The best thoughts often come in the
morning after waking

Busy people do not have the time
or energy to worry about the
triviality of other people

Look for the circumstances you want

To achieve great things we must live
as though we are never going
to die

Do not make the day shorter by
waking up late

Genius is the faculty of doing a thing
that nobody supposed could be
done at all

Try not to leave words unsaid and
deeds undone

People look different naked than with their clothes on

Respect your body's needs

Learn the luxury of doing good

A person makes a name, not a name the person

Friendship is like wine: the older it gets, the better it is

The truth is never simple

The surest way to get a thing in life is to be prepared for doing without it

The difference between the right word and the almost right word is the difference between lightning and the lightning bug (Mark Twain)

There is happiness in the most disagreeable duty when you realize you're getting it out of the way

Let fear help in the decision-making process, not hurt

Respect yourself and others

Live out loud

Look at the bright side of things

Why despair when sadness is
sufficient

Praise in public, criticize in private

It's not your job to get people to
like you

Aim for success, not perfection

Perform whatever you promise

Reading makes a full man and
writing an exact man
(Francis Bacon)

Do not fret over old griefs

The show must go on

Grasp a little and you may secure it;
grasp too much and you will lose
everything

What's done is done

Remember the power of kindness

Do not learn useless things

If you do not love yourself, then you
cannot love others

Find solutions to life's puzzles

Everyone lays a burden on the
willing horse

Seeking to please others is
a perilous trap

Be indifferent to the world in
which you are different from
everyone else

Learn the history of your town

When you lose, learn a lesson

Only lazy people get bored

Begin each day with your
favorite music

Calmness is a great advantage

Most failures come from within

The creative instinct is an enormous
super energy which no single life
can consume (Pearl Buck)

No person is good enough to govern
another without that person's
consent

It is easy to judge someone when you
do not know him

Faith can move mountains

Out of the mouths of babes come
great truths

Better to keep peace than to make
peace

You may hate the things a person
does, but never hate the person

Let the quality of your deeds speak
on your behalf

To know, you must do

Living life to its fullest potential is
living life

Do not die with any unmet dreams

Spend more time living rather than
getting ready to live

Neither an egg nor an ego is any
good until you break it

You do not have all that you have all
the time

A day cannot have a price tag

Follow through on promises

Be responsible for your own
happiness

Better a friendly refusal than
an unwilling promise

The mind is slow in unlearning what it has been long in learning

Do not part with your illusions

Anything that lasts only a short time is not worth making a lifetime of sacrifices for

Experience your feelings

Recognize opportunities

Lost time is never found again (Benjamin Franklin)

Watch what happens to a wagon when one wheel comes off

There is plenty of success to be spread around to a lot of people

The mind is like a TV set: when it goes blank, it is a good idea to turn off the sound

The best way to cheer up yourself is cheer up somebody else

Nothing is so infectious as example

Find the extraordinary in the ordinary

Personality is to the man what perfume is to the flower

Find your purpose

A little uncertainty is good

Even a fool is right sometimes

Exciting times can sometimes
   become a little dangerous

Words have the power to destroy
   or heal

Make the most of yourself

If you think you are free,
   then you are

He who digs a pit for another
   may fall into it himself

No one can tell you how to live
   your life

Ears are not made to shut,
   but a mouth is

Compete; do not envy

If you want to see how little you
   actually know, then read
   a dictionary

Wise people understand that they
   will make mistakes

Give to charity

Advise not what is pleasant but what is useful

Do things quietly and at a slower pace

Take a vacation at home

Understand what bothers you

Buy while you can get it

Avoid people who deliberately hurt you

Small deeds are better than big intentions

When you win, nothing hurts

Taking initiative makes one a creator

Read cheerful and inspiring books

It is better to ask some questions than to know all the answers (James Thurber)

Some things you never get used to

The only person you can really correct and change is yourself

Nothing enters into a closed hand

The benefits are great when a family eats together

A person is defined by what he makes of himself during his lifetime

Never subtract from your character to add to your popularity

Old things can bring new discoveries

Forgiving someone means that you are also forgetting what she did

Enjoy life's pleasures

Wear comfortable shoes

Good things come in small packages

Do not get off the merry-go-round before it stops

Don't talk unless you can improve the silence

Reality is not an illusion

It is difficult to leave a good thing

Your education is not complete when you finish school

Misunderstanding is no excuse

Truth does not blush

Life is the greatest bargain: we get it for nothing

Don't take out your frustrations on
the people you love the most

Don't take the wrong side of an
argument just because your
opponent has taken the right side

Make the first move

Bring more love and truth into
the world

Live richly

Simple words can have profound
meanings

Wisdom is to the soul what health is
to the body

Learn to accept events with
intelligence

Admit your mistakes

An insatiable curiosity keeps
you young

Give a man a fish and you feed him
for a day; teach a man to fish
and you feed him for a lifetime
(Chinese proverb)

Pain does not last forever

Honesty is the best policy

Our humility and open-mindedness
   make us teachable

Find some good in everything

The most certain sign of wisdom
   is a positive outlook

A life examined and explored is a life
   worth living

Give honest and sincere appreciation

Don't give too much weight to
   erudition alone

A good reputation cannot be bought
   for any amount of money

Watch sunrises

The more effort, the more notice

Believe that you are gifted for
   something

Do not pet a porcupine unless you
   are looking for trouble

Keep a tight rein on your temper

Do not cut down the tree that gives
   you shade

Loneliness is curable

It is the little things in life that count

Seize good luck

A person's thoughts are within her own power

Death is a necessity of life

Use your powers for good

Present neglect makes future regret

Fill the now

Win some victory for humanity

People were built to adjust

Think big

If you don't get the better of yourself, someone will

Riches enlarge rather than satisfy appetites

It is better to be ready and not go than to be not ready and go

Jealousy leads to folly and injustice

Hypocrisy is part of human nature

Make your home a refuge from the rest of the world

A person is as big as the things that
make him mad

The world is your oyster

Don't use food as a compensation for
what is missing in your life

Music tells us about the times we
live in

Follow love and it will flee; flee love
and it will follow you

Manners make the man

People who would not think of
talking with their mouths
full often speak with their
heads empty

Know what you can control and
what you can't

Things and people are not what we
wish them to be; they are what
they are

Truth surfaces like oil on water

Charm is a way of getting a yes
without asking a question

Courtesy never goes out of style

Bad people are usually not happy

There is no such thing as fun for
    the whole family

Laughter is a pain reliever

Read more books

The future is always more expensive

A solved problem should no longer
    bother you

Before honor is humility

Life is made up of little things

Fix your own faults before you ask
    others to fix theirs

A jack of all trades is a master
    of none

You go further when you know
    where you are going

Better to turn back than to lose
    your way

Talk quietly

Compliment parents of well-behaved
    children

There are only two classes: first class
    and no class

Don't say "I can"; say "I will"

If you enjoy old age, then you have
won the game

Test your endurance

You can judge a society by how it
treats its children

A person with vision sees the
invisible

There are no free lunches

Memorize a poem

Compare what you deserve with
what you have, and you'll
be happy

You cannot be smarter than everyone

Better one good friend than many
acquaintances

Reach for the impossible

Strive for excellence

Stay involved in things that are
important to you

Don't answer the phone just because
it is ringing

There's good in everybody

Beware the anger of a patient man

It is better to delay than to err

Hear the evidence before you pass
    sentence

Good friends should bring out
    the best in you

Make tough choices and accept
    the consequences

Better an open enemy than
    a false friend

Remember to write thank-you notes

Some decisions will give you joy or
    heartache for a lifetime

Wisdom often consists of knowing
    what to do next

We are never more discontented
    with others than when we are
    discontented with ourselves

Be the best judge of yourself

Having a little is the best way to
    having a lot

Intelligent people possess a certain
    skepticism to them

A willing heart sees nothing as
    impossible

Invention breeds invention

We forget others' troubles faster than
we do our own

If there is no laughter in a day,
then the day is wasted

True beauty does not need to
dress up

We have the freedom to choose
to act constructively or, when
appropriate, do nothing at all

Wisdom is seldom used during
troubled times

Keep some opinions to yourself

Obey the speed limit

Remember your pleasures with
gratitude

Don't argue with someone
who is right

Live frugally

Happiness does not consist
in things, but in thoughts

Every habit and faculty is preserved
and increased by correspondent
actions

The covetous person is his own
    tormentor

Hang loose

Success is never final and failure
    is never fatal

Learn by doing

Return always to what is essential
    and worthy

There can be light in darkness

Do not fight a battle if there is
    nothing to win

Eat when you are hungry

Feed your mind as well as your body

Lawmakers should not be
    lawbreakers

Praise every improvement,
    even the slightest one

Do not let trifles disturb you

Too many fingers spoil the pie

Deal gracefully with rejection

Become more sensitive to your
    vulnerabilities

Those who have not tasted the
   bitterest of life's bitters cannot
   appreciate the sweetest of
   life's sweets

Something is kept when you give

A moment on the lips, a lifetime
   on the hips

The way a person lives is a way
   to judge a person's character

Every day should be a new
   experience

Interesting parents raise interesting
   children

Be humble and patient

Change brings new opportunities

Do not marry someone who has more
   problems than you

Speak fair and think what you will

He who considers too much will
   perform little

Luck is the residue of design

Take a moment to meditate

Everything happens for a good
   reason

On an unknown path every foot
is slow

Do not complain of the boat that
carries you safely

Beauty is everywhere, take
a good look

There's many a good tune played on
an old fiddle

Half the world does not know how
the other half lives

Better to feel pity than be pitied

Stop trying to change people

A friend's success should not make
you feel like a failure

Goodness comes from within

Nothing is as powerful as the
moment a person learns
something on his own

Instead of opening your mouth,
open your eyes

Action generates inspiration

To fit in, take the tone of the
company you are with

History judges all things in time

Do more with less

Wise people know how to
     keep money

Give your emotions room to breathe

Never sleep apart from your spouse
     unless you have to

A perfect dwelling always finds
     an inhabitant

You cannot hang everything on
     one nail

Eat to live, don't live to eat

Thank your lucky stars

Take advantage of the opportunities
     that are presented to you

Half an orange tastes as sweet
     as a whole one

Never stop exploring

Surround yourself with things that
     make you smile

Adversity discovers virtue

Relationships can wear out

Speak of the devil and he is bound
     to appear

See the miraculous in the commonplace (Henry David Thoreau)

A person's discontent is his worst evil

If you bake bread with indifference, you bake a bitter bread that feeds no man's hunger

A bargain is not a bargain unless you can use the product

Learning has no limit

If you love someone, set him free

Just begin

Words can be art

Categorizing people is destructive and unfair

Don't compare your present lover with past ones

Needs can be met if understood

How you give is just as important as what you give

Do not look forward to the day when you will stop suffering—because then you will be dead

It is easy to live life when everything
    is going well

Cut your losses

From each according to his abilities,
    to each according to his needs

A busy life has no time for quarrels

Inspiration is all around you

A tree is known by its fruit

Reinvent your world

The characteristic that brings a
    person to the top is usually the
    same thing that brings her back
    down, too

It takes less time to avoid an
    accident than it does to report it

In the simple doing of tasks there is
    sacredness

Love is a pleasurable process

Cultivate peace and harmony
    with all

Learn to labor and wait
    (Henry Wadsworth Longfellow)

Cultivate your garden

You must do a crazy thing once in a while to keep from going nuts

Go whole hog

Opportunity sometimes knocks very softly

When you open a door, you do not know how many rooms lie beyond

Nobody roots for Goliath

A successful relationship needs both people believing in each other

Realize that there are other points of view

Visualize good things happening to you

Your unknown territory may be someone else's home

Great leaders earn their credentials during difficult times

Grow old gracefully

Accept the good and run with it

Before you can move others, you must be moved

Try to see the other person's point of view first

Be on time

Appreciate your odd moments

No one is ever really normal

Hope can be the best medicine

Apply your full energy to the project
at hand

Never promise a fish until it
is caught

Seek out the good in people

See things fresh

Love breaks the rule of common
sense

Get the facts

Do as you would be done by

Friendship is gained by listening
instead of talking

Don't be discouraged by your
mistakes

Do not play with fire

Deeds are better than promises

Work hard so you can enjoy the
simple pleasures of life

Many a fine estate has a fence,
but also a gate and a key

Beauty is only skin deep

Find a private haven

The best advice is, don't give it

Become what you have to

If you wait until retirement to start
living, you have waited too long

A house is defined by the character
of the people who live in it and
visit it

The more a child feels valued,
the better his values will be

Feel too young to get old

Tact consists of knowing how far
to go

When a conversation begins, decide
whether you should hear the
other person or that the other
person should hear you

Some people never learn

People gossip about things they are
interested in

Look twice before you leap
    (Charlotte Brontë)

Don't do anything that conflicts with
    common sense

The prettiest flowers bloom the
    shortest period

It is easy to live a bad life

Reality is a collective hunch

Bring something to the table

Faith is a show of strength

Often your faith in an uncertain
    result is the only thing that
    gets results

To be content with little is true
    happiness

Write plain, simple English

The slow times would not be
    enjoyable if you did not have
    the fast times

Alter ideas and you alter the world

We can either change our actions
    or change our beliefs about
    those actions

Be kind to the unkind

Channel your anxiety toward
performance

Do not be a mouse or the cat
will eat you

Two captains will sink a ship

No one can censure your thoughts

A person's real worth is determined
by what he does when he has
nothing to do

We become by example

Rain never melted anyone

Open yourself to new experiences

Endure pain with dignity

Don't preach to the choir

Life is 10 percent what happens
to you and 90 percent how you
react to it

Start something today

Make much out of little

Life can be beautiful

You'll find growth among those who
don't agree with you

Fear plays a big part in our lives

Thin ice and thick ice look the same from a distance

It is easier to give advice about something once you have been through it yourself

Be your own best friend

Walking on a dirt road in the country does wonders for your soul

Education takes a lifetime

Buy in bulk

Flattery is nice, but do not fall in love with it

Create rituals of things you look forward to doing on a regular basis

Anyone who says raising children is not the most difficult job in the world is not doing it right

As long as we have freedom of the press, we have freedom

Straighten out your problems before you go to bed and wake up smiling

Good times are for remembering

Simple wants are easily supplied

Thinking too much about the future
makes the present unpleasant

Just looking at nature from a
mountaintop is the best prize

A good book is a great friend

Perception is truth

Simply doing nothing does not avoid
risk, but heightens it

Even the longest day will come
to an end

Living in itself is risky

Say things well

Excellence is achieved through
concentration

There is no elevator to success—
only stairs

Make service an integral part
of your life

Simple will always be in style

You are born a genius or not; what
you do with that genius is a sign
of character and talent

It takes years to build trust, but only seconds to destroy it

A pig is beautiful to another pig

Do not look where you fell, but where you slipped

Life is an opportunity to benefit from

Obstacles make the goal clearer

There are always plenty of people and things to love

Ignorance of the law is no excuse

Cut out the details that fritter away what is most valuable in life

Troubles can strengthen your appreciation of life

Clearly assess your strengths and weaknesses

History teaches by example

A person is as great as her thoughts

If you get off track, get back on as fast as you can

Try really hard

A most unlikely stranger can become a friend

Surrender to love

The pleasure of what we enjoy is lost
by coveting more

Thinking of yesterday should not use
up too much of today

Faith is stronger than hope

Life's possibilities are endless

Build a simple wardrobe

Associate yourself with only
trustworthy people

Those who know do not speak; those
who speak do not know

Arguments usually end when one
person does not want to argue
anymore

When someone lets you down,
don't give up on him

Exercise instead of worry

Anger improves nothing but the arch
of a cat's back

Offer hope

To persevere is to win

Health is the greatest of human
blessings

A little impatience spoils great plans

Always leave home with a tender
good-bye and loving words

Dry your clothes in the sun

Do not do what is already done

Make your imagination real

Be skeptical and tolerant

When we are in trouble, dwelling on
it does not really help

A bully is always a coward

Use your weaknesses

Memories are your most valuable
possessions

Great love and great achievements
involve great risk

Turn your dreams into reality

You do not need an invitation to
help others

Inspiration gives direction

Strength comes from commitment

Ambition is putting a ladder against
the sky

Keep realistic expectations

A good habit is a lot easier to learn
than a bad habit is to break

Do your own useful work without
regard to the honor or admiration
your efforts might win from
others

If you think you can, you can

Don't air your dirty laundry

Worrying shows that you care

The reverse side also has
a reverse side

Life is too precious; do not destroy it

It is nice to be important, but it is
more important to be nice

Most possessions are used to impress
others rather than to serve a
unique function

To each his own

If the wilderness is not protected, it
will not be able to protect you

If you want to keep a secret, keep it
to yourself

Say something every day to
encourage your children

Strength makes life easier

A good friendship can get you
through many a hard time

Stand behind your decisions

By keeping active you slow down
the aging process

It is okay to cry

A small garden is just as beautiful
as a large one

Control the menu of thoughts and
images that flash through your
mind

A good deed shines in a naughty
world

Belittle others to be little

Even legends die

Love funny stories

The ideal we embrace is our
better self

Wealth isn't necessarily success

Your strengths are already in place
and can be nurtured

If only one knows it, it is secret;
if two know it, it is public

Every dog has his day

You cannot lose what you do
not have

The best way to stay healthy
is to eat properly and exercise

Be genuinely interested in the lives
of your friends

If it sounds good to the ears, then it
is good music

The person with big dreams is more
powerful than one with all the
facts

Be your child's greatest advocate

Wherever you go, there you are

Finish projects before they are due

Share the credit

Economy is the easy chair of old age

It is good practice to look back before
   you move forward

Create your own world

Giving eliminates taking

Nobody knows everything

Throughout history, there will be
   only one of you

How you spend your time is how you
   live your life

Question everything to get to
   the truth

There is no harm in asking

Scratch where it itches

Every person is unique

Reading is exercise for the mind

Enlarge your consciousness

An investment in knowledge pays
   the best interest

Nature is a better artist than man

It is hard to carry a full cup evenly

You learn to love others by how you
   love yourself

Life is an uncertain voyage

Take your fun where you find it

The last chicken is the hardest
to catch

Pure beauty exists when the head
and heart work together

Nothing can prepare you for love

Don't take good health for granted

Direct love away from yourself
toward others

Life is a big canvas, so throw all
the paint on it you can

Expend your energy for excellence

Try not to merely react in
the moment

You can have success and serenity
at the same time

Life is tough, but you can be tougher

Friendships should never be painful
to keep up

Pray more with your heart and less
with your brain

The earth was here before mankind

A balanced life needs to combine
the past, present, and future

Beware of advice based on someone's
fears

Nature is a great inspiration

Death is the only thing that can
come between true friends

Faith is truth to the person who
has faith

Misery loves company

Rejoice in life

Great people fail as often as ordinary
people

Free your weekends for your family

Let your anger out in safe action

Stretch your boundaries

Make reason your guide

Perseverance is failing ten times and
succeeding the eleventh

You gain strength, courage, and
confidence every time you look
fear in the face

Tomorrow is a new day

Good looks can sometimes be
a nuisance

Learn how to make and keep
good friends

If we take care of the earth, it will
take care of us

Nostalgia is always reflected with
the knowledge we have now

Time should be spent solving
problems, not worrying about
them

Everyone is selling something

Most people are better judges of
others than they are of
themselves

Most things do not work without
some glitches

Motion is not necessarily action

Where there is smoke, there is fire

Doing nothing is harder than
doing something

Acts indicate intentions

Decide who you want to become

Finish every day and be done with it

Stick up for yourself

Be nice to people on your way up because you'll meet them on your way down

Be receptive; everyone's life is interesting

Who would wish to be valued must make himself scarce

Avoid anyone named Honest John

Reading a good book is like spending time with a dear friend

When you think all is lost, the future remains

Apologize when appropriate

Don't become too big for your britches

Grow with friends

Chalk it up to experience

Know your own faults as well as you know others' faults

When time is wasted, life is wasted

People act differently in a crowd than when they are alone

You are never nearing the end of your problems

Pleasure is gained by giving

Respect other people's choices

You cannot build character and courage by taking away another's initiative and independence

Learn how to distinguish between cheap thrills and meaningful, lasting rewards

A good cookbook never gets outdated

Make a contribution

If you learn something for the third time, it would be wise to remember it

Laugh with, but never laugh at

Promote yourself but do not demote another

It is better to be a good person and fulfill your obligations than to have renown and power

It is easy to condemn something not understood

The truth is in you

Discipline yourself to save money

Affection is never wasted

Inspired work is thrilling

Avoid what you see others doing
wrong

Look for ways to be more useful

Listen to your favorite music while
paying bills

It is better to help out a friend than
to be helped out by a friend

Reading a good book is like taking
a journey

Action first, prayer second

He who overcomes others is strong;
he who overcomes himself is
mightier still

A watched pot never boils

Play it cool

Receive by giving

Good acts should be addictive

Most of life's events are unexpected

Peace is goodwill in action

Find the right solution for
the problem

All great things in life are achieved
with passion

Pursue more than just pleasure

Never forget a kindness

Teach yourself how to think, not
what to think

Every season of the year has its high
points and low points

Never invest money you cannot
afford to lose

Do not fear fewer tomorrows

Develop all your senses

Don't be a rubber stamp

Give yourself plenty of time to play

Allow yourself to feel rich without
money

Sweep the dirt from the front of your
own door and do not worry about
your neighbor's

It is easy to live in the world;
it is difficult to change it

Times change and we with time

The whole ocean is made up
of little drops

Live your affirmations

Live each day as it comes

Some people think about the same
thought a thousand times while
others think a thousand different
thoughts

Don't confuse comfort with happiness

Through vigilance we can forestall
the tendency to excess

Friends slowly won are long held

To make enemies, talk; to make
friends, listen

It is easier to make friends than it is
to keep them

Do not look too far into the future

Don't try to take on a new
personality; it does not work

If you want something done, ask a
busy person (Benjamin Franklin)

With every deed you're sowing a seed

Concentrate on your strengths
instead of dwelling on your
weaknesses

Think and your mind will stay fresh

Believe in what you can become

Time determines who is right

Become who you want to become

Delaying can be dangerous

Compose yourself

Take a wider view

Not all people can look good in all
clothes

Our capacities are greater than
we imagine

Animals cannot tell jokes

Virtue is enough

Laughter is a tranquilizer with no
side effects

Nature knows her business better
than we do

Pay off your mortgage early
if possible

It costs more to do ill than to do well

Don't carry grudges

The past does not determine
the future

Falling is a part of learning

It's one thing to talk of bulls, it's
another to be in the bullring

Understanding creates tolerance

Know what to remember as well as
what to forget

Resist fear

Be expressive

Ask others about themselves

Be a self-starter

Liars usually have good memories
because they need to remember
their lies

A good listener is a silent flatterer

Every compromise is surrender and
invites new demands

Children and grandparents have
a common enemy—the parents

Adapt or perish

Anyone can be happy during good
times, but only the strong can
be happy in bad times

Beam with pride when your children
accomplish something

Do everything in order

Profit from valuable lessons

Intelligence is like a river: the deeper
it is, the less noise it makes

Use your head for something
besides a hat rack

Be aware of others' motives

It is amazing how much good
you can do if you do not
care who gets the credit

The fear of losing is diminished
when you lose for the first time
and survive

Gifts cannot take the place of neglect

An artist does not know when she is
going to paint a masterpiece

Understanding life is a lifelong goal

Choose your love, then love
your choice

Enjoy the spirit of the unusual

The past is the only part of your life that you cannot change

"Almost" only counts in horseshoes

One is innocent until proven guilty

There is no dress rehearsal for life

Do not confuse sex with love and intimacy

Don't fish for strawberries in the bottom of the sea

It takes a thief to catch a thief

Get out of the house every day

Hit 'em where they ain't

Frustration is generally vented toward the weak

It is easier to fight with a family member than a friend, but it is also easier to make up with a family member than a friend

Speak well of the dead

It is okay to feel sorry for yourself— for five minutes

Hope keeps the heart from breaking

Get what you can, and what you get, hold

Remember the good of your past more than the bad

Halving your wants quadruples your wealth

Go with the odds

Time doesn't change things; you actually have to change them yourself

Make art

There is potential for growth in every mistake we make

Be happy when conscience hurts you; be worried when it doesn't

Don't let them scare you

Learn to take the right roads in life

If you are going to do something wrong, at least enjoy it

Knowing that you do not know much is knowing a lot

Forgive your enemies, but never forget their names

Love has no ceiling

Lost time is never found again

Teach your kids about money

Fearing death does not make it
easier to live life

Never be ashamed to own up to
a wrong

You are here now

A thankful heart is a great virtue

If you make yourself a doormat,
you will be stepped on

Save only things you will need to
refer to or want to read again

Disappointment hurts more
than pain

Buy comfortable furniture

Out of your vulnerabilities will come
your strength

Nature is a great teacher

A drawback to success is that it
offers very little time for personal
pursuits

All important truths are simple

Do not set up boundaries for yourself

It is easier to argue something
   knowing that you are right

Try never to embarrass your children

Nothing is lost when you seek
   the truth

The world is your cow, but you have
   to do the milking

Do not try to fix your life all at once

Give your hearts, but not into each
   other's keeping

No matter what you attain in life,
   you are still only a person

It is easier to dump the cart than
   to load it

If you are bored, look for something
   to do

If at first you do not succeed,
   try again

Believe that you have no barriers

Just be yourself

If you are patient, you can
   eventually accomplish anything

A beaten path is a safe one

Avoid investing events with power or
meaning they don't have

Discover something that you would
die for

Abundance, like want, ruins many

Sometimes, there is a fine line
between laughing and crying

Successful people believe that
they are destined for great things

The more you know, the less you fear

Good things do not have to last a
long time

Focus your energies on the present

A happy heart runs like a good
machine

We are not meant to fly solo

If you want to learn about
something, then watch
it very carefully

Shared experiences make great
conversation

The most important thing a parent
can do for the children is to love
the other parent

Nothing can destroy the beauty of the center of the soul

The end doesn't always justify the means

Call things by their right names

If you give more, then you have more to give

The meaning of life is to find meaning

The best time to make friends is before you need them

A machine running is worth two standing still

Duty before pleasure

A man's character is his fate

Be comfortable with not knowing

The best questions have more than one answer

Don't let being tired stop you

Be forgiving of yourself and others

In life, things don't have a particular order to follow

Change is the only thing that is
   permanent

Rome was not built in a day

Even when you have pains, you don't
   have to be a pain

Bait the hook well; the fish will bite

Lies are the hardest things to forgive

Single steps add up to a completed
   goal

It is an art to thoroughly enjoy
   solitude

Do not count your chickens before
   they hatch

Support candidates you believe in

If you cannot be kind, at least
   be vague

Never put off till tomorrow what you
   can do today

Keep the home fires burning

Floss your teeth

Don't just "drop in" on people

Enjoy what you have to do

Give yourself fully to your endeavors

He who sows courtesy reaps friendship

Passion for life leads to a passionate life

Until you do something, most people believe that you cannot do it

Conquer ignorance

Intelligence seeks its own level

Do little things well

Don't blame others; take responsibility for your life

Place a high value on yourself and then prove that you are worth it

Learn how to receive love

Life is a great bundle of little things

Tomorrow will become a yesterday

Choose a business partner who is strong where you are weak

People take advantage of your weaknesses

Meet your obligations

Success is being able to spend your life in your own way

Two birds in the bush are still two
    birds in the bush

Wish for only what you want

Treat others like you want to
    be treated

Hear both sides before judging

Talk slowly, think quickly

Become a possibilitarian

No change in circumstances will
    change a defect in character

Avoid electronic overload

Keep on living right up until the
    time you die

Events are impersonal

Play the hand that's dealt you

Quiet the mind

Crises tap into strength that you did
    not know was there

When you discover you are on the
    wrong path, turn back

Guilt is a powerful emotion

All's well that ends well

One day at a time

Maintaining your good character is easier than trying to regain it

Begin all actions with a thought

One should respect knowledge, but doubt is what gets you an education

Don't get lost to whim

Faith and self-respect lead to an outward serenity and inward peace

The happiest person is the person who thinks the most interesting thoughts

The greatest result of education is tolerance

Get out of debt

Luck affects everything

Understand your role

Enthusiasm is obvious to everyone

Our lives are meant to be lived

Life is an emotional journey

Not what we give but what we share makes us great

A certain style of clothes makes you
look more attractive

Do not look at problems as stumbling
blocks but as stepping-stones

The majority can be wrong

The toughest part of being on a diet
is shutting up about it

Look beyond the past, present,
and future

The value of money lies in what
we do with it

You can

Pack your own parachute

Look at life from your own unique
perspective

Necessity makes decision making
easy

Now is a good time to begin living
your dreams

If things look hopeless, look to see if
you are not facing the wrong
direction

Truth is a jewel of many facets

Determine not to waste your time and attention on mindless blather

All misfortune is but a stepping-stone to fortune

Even certainty is not certain

Some people learn nothing and forget everything

Good communications make sense of a lot of things

When you have power, you spend most of your time trying to protect it

Life is what your thoughts make it

It is easy to betray yourself

Imagination is for rehearsing dreams and reliving joys

Don't spend your time waiting

Breaking bad habits is the hardest thing to learn how to do

Stand behind your decisions

Take time to choose the words you live by

Takers lose and givers win

When you betray someone else,
   you also betray yourself

Make new friends in every period
   of your life

Never go grocery shopping when
   you are hungry

Keep your accomplishments in
   perspective

If you think about something too
   much, you will probably not do it

Make the best of a bad situation

Being who you are and having people
   perceive you as who you are are
   two distinct things

When you plant a flower garden, you
   show people that you care about
   more than just yourself

Choose to experience life

Starting to do something is the
   hardest part of doing something

Pay attention to the small details of
   your conduct

A little bait catches a large fish

Whenever you choose to be alone,
a world opens up to you

You can never plan the future by
the past

You can be strict and loving at the
same time

Great vacations are usually too short

All the advice and wisdom cannot
help you until you apply it daily

Your body is the harp of your soul

Gather knowledge, insight, and
experience and then make your
own decision

Look for opportunities

If you play both ends against the
middle, the middle will fold up

Love has a tragic side

Praise in others what you would like
to have praised in you

Cream always rises to the top

Fads are meant to die

It is better to suffer injustice than
to do it

When speaking sincerely, do not
    think of the words too long

Live in the present

Remain calm

If you have a loving family,
    it is amazing what you
    can do without

A wise person knows that she cannot
    know everything

The nail that sticks up gets
    hammered down

Encourage self-sufficiency

Love is the only thing okay to do
    in excess

People should be judged from where
    they stand, not from where you
    stand

Fall seven times, stand up eight

People will meet the expectations
    that you set for them

Nothing of value is lost by taking
    your time

Enjoy the life you are given

Don't be afraid of tomorrow

You can't have everything; where
would you put it?

If you want to get somewhere,
know where you are going

Push your life to a higher level

Wisdom does not come by chance

Ask for advice when you need it

The sun will set without your
assistance

No one should fear the truth

Be the first to forgive

Always look for the silver lining

Happiness is a by-product of a
thoughtful, disciplined life

All that is out there is not all that
is known

Seeking revenge prevents the wound
from healing

It is hard to be a hero for a long time

Sometimes the truth is not simple

It is better to light one candle than
to curse the darkness

Great friendships last until the grave

A new broom sweeps the cleanest

Nature does not distinguish between good and evil

Don't let assumptions keep you awake nights

Remember there are two sides to every story

He is wise who can make a friend of a foe

It is no disgrace to fall down—the disgrace is in not getting up and going ahead

You can change your attitude

Follow your bliss

Live according to your nature

The more we help others, the more we help ourselves

What you are thinking about, you are becoming

The best way to make your dreams come true is to wake up (Paul-Toussaint-Jules Valéry)

You cannot please all of the people all of the time

Worry gives you something to do, but doesn't get you anywhere

Forgiving someone has obvious benefits to both parties

Practice seeing things as they are

Life is experimental

Imagine great things

Some problems baffle even the wisest people

It is impossible to teach without learning something yourself

If you have a voice, sing

Every day surround yourself with beauty

A person who does not know what he is good at will not be sure what he is good for

Tact is the ability to see other people as they think you see them

See things for what they really are

An imagination can make reality more enjoyable

Drive away fear

Throw out everything but the aspirin

You don't really know a person until you live with him

The greatest fault is to be conscious of none

Worrying can be controlled

You cannot buy life

Anticipate what your opponents will do

You cannot prepare for chance

Once you are interested in a subject, attack it

It is easier to accept love than it is to give it

Be a lifter, not a leaner

Listen to silence

Prayer hinders no work

No great man ever complains of want of opportunity

A person's pride and fortune usually rise and fall together

Happiness is always sweet and short

Keep an eye on what you want

Knowledge enables man to work
more intelligently and effectively

You are not your job

You cannot improve the past, but you
can improve the future

Let go of projects that don't feel
rewarding

Nature is the best teacher of change

An original mind is rarely
understood

Wisdom is sometimes disguised
as foolishness

Pause and reflect

Be patient with everyone

Discover creative solitude

Life is a coin you can only spend
once

Do not get behind the eight ball

An apple a day keeps the doctor
away

Count your change

A good soldier never looks behind
him

Keep life simple

Visualize it

Stop blaming others for your failures

By making waves, you find where
your course lies

God has a sense of humor

Laugh in the face of disaster

You cannot spoil a rotten egg

The night appears to last longer than
the day

Make the most of your regrets

Trust smartly

An open ear and a closed mouth
is the best-known substitution
for wisdom

Do it well; you may not get a second
chance

Activities give life quality

People can surprise you

Enjoy money while you have it

Share your favorite recipes

How you say something is as
important as what you say

Certain things are right at different times of your life

The quieter you become, the more you can hear

Know all that you are capable of learning

Living well is the best revenge

Life is just one damn thing after another

Knowledge is a precious treasure that cannot be given away nor stolen

Making money is easier than keeping it

Gardening is cheaper than therapy

Don't wait to give to charity

A good speech will make the audience laugh, cry, and think

Keep your travel kit packed and ready

People with tact have less to retract

Respect those who can be of no possible value to you

Never use profanity

Don't dismiss a good idea just
because you don't like where
it came from

Money was made to be shared

Expect adversity

The art of writing is that of applying
the seat of the pants to the seat
of the chair

If you like yourself, then you will like
other people, too

When you decide to begin, begin
right away

A forgiving person has many friends

Hear as well as be heard

If you don't toot your own horn,
no one else will toot it for you

Let your children go if you want to
keep them

To find out what someone is like,
find out what she does in her
spare time

The world looks different at night
than it does during the day

Create your own luck

After you climb to the top of the wall,
don't kick over the ladder

Patience wins all the time

Pursue happiness

You will never regret doing extra
work

Good things can remain in our
hearts long after they have ended

Freedom is not easily attained

Start getting up an hour earlier

Always carry something to do in case
you have to wait

Understanding more is not
necessarily better

Better to be a person's last romance
than his first one

Good fortune is usually the result of
wisdom and hard work, not luck

Philosophers discover more than
they solve

Little and often fills the purse

Every minute of every day, the sun is
always shining somewhere

Reaching old age is a form of
   winning

True relaxation is an art

Life changes in unpredictable ways

Make your communications so clear
   that an honest person could
   not misunderstand them and
   a dishonest person could not
   misrepresent you

Happy memories get better over time

Neighbors make the neighborhood

If two ride on a horse, one must
   ride behind

Genius begins great works; labor
   alone finishes them

Listening will bring harmony to your
   family

Education begins at home

Common sense is rarely common

More learning occurs outside of
   school than inside

Show respect for others' time

Get it in writing

A thing of beauty is a joy forever
(John Keats)

Stick to your guns

You can tell a person's intelligence
within five minutes of meeting
her

Right behind the need for food,
clothing, and shelter is the
need to work

Only death destroys hope

Be happy with what you have while
working for what you want

Learn things from your enemies

Get people to take you seriously

Your home should not feel like a
birdcage and you like a bird

Kindness is the sunshine of
social life

If you enjoy being a guest, you must
sometimes be a host

When "if" and "when" are planted,
"nothing" grows

A journey of a thousand miles must
begin with a single step

No lies are white; they are all black

The beginning of something is
usually the best part of it

Refuse to be negative

Accept challenges

Kiss someone good night even if he is
already asleep

If you remembered everything,
you would have no time to
do new things

Get up and go

The only thing you can be sure
of improving is yourself

Imperfections can make
things perfect

Respect time

Better alone than in bad company

Leave the herd and think for yourself

Learn to make good choices

Keep your shirt on

Do not be disturbed at trifles

Be grateful for what you have
learned

The young look more attractive flirting than the old

Comments made "off the record" seldom stay there

It is all in how you take it

One minute of keeping your mouth shut is worth an hour's explanation

Don't dissect things too much

Practice listening to your body and trusting what it reveals

Falling in love is exciting

It is harder to climb the mountain than to climb down

They conquer who believe they can (Ralph Waldo Emerson)

A home is made of love and dreams

Thinking is the exercise for the mind

Your memories make you wealthy or poor

Dare to be unexpected

You cannot steal second base and keep one foot on first

Practice increases knowledge

Always leave something to wish for

There is no defect except from within

Never say never

One good idea put to use is worth a
    hundred buzzing around in the
    back of your head

Industry will improve great talents

Worry often gives a small thing
    a big shadow

An innkeeper's job looks easy when
    you dream of owning an inn

It is easier to stay out than get out

Eventually everything gets done

Nature abhors a vacuum

Freedom has responsibility

Conserve energy

Strong lives are motivated by
    dynamic purposes

Famous people are not necessarily
    good people

A beautiful picture is a silent teacher

Every good has its evil

Do good to others

When you begin something, believe it
will end positively

New opinions and thoughts are
the hardest ones to accept

Take time to turn yourself around

Not everyone should know how
you feel

Big lies are usually more believable
than small ones

In between the ideal and the possible
lies life

Talk to your plants and animals

Be cautious of the lowest bid

There is a whole universe beyond
Earth

A big problem is a small problem
that was never handled

Search others for their virtues,
yourself for your vices

Don't consent to creep when you feel
an impulse to soar

Successful parenting utilizes good
management

The hardest part about
    creating art is beginning

Buy a toy for yourself

Don't believe everything you hear
    or read

Your job should bear the imprint
    of your personality

From a short pleasure comes a long
    repentance

The best defense is a good offense

Don't do at night what you'd shun
    in broad daylight

Love never grows tired

Secret charity and secret patience
    are best

Dreaming about the next day saves
    you preparation time

Keep out of debt and you will keep
    out of trouble

Think of retirement as being
    a teenager again

Families can either cause great
    happiness or tremendous sorrow

Everyone is changed by the future

Always toss a coin in a wishing well

Remember the good decisions
you made

Optimism is a gift

Look up, not down

Never judge before you see

Most lies begin as the truth

A fish would not get caught if it kept
its mouth shut

There is a big difference between
action and words

Stand up for your high principles,
even if you're alone

You can't take it with you

With each step taken, you get closer
to your goal

You are as good as your genes

Use honesty without priggishness

Whoever cares to learn will always
find a teacher

Keep expectations in check

Read things with different points of
view and try to learn something

We all play a part in life

Windows are to look out from,
not into

Play with your heart

When you fight with a brother or
sister, you are hurting yourself,
because he or she is a part of you

Do not negotiate out of fear

Everyone enjoys himself in his
own way

Stolen kisses are the best

We become strong only after we have
acknowledged our weaknesses

Be wise in misfortune

It is not the answer that enlightens,
but the question

Go in peace

The fire of a past love will always
burn with a little flame

Be inspired by curious things

Appetite comes with eating

Talk about more than just the
weather

A good night's sleep can cure many an ill

A person generally does not think the same at twenty as at forty

Bloom where you are planted

Sometimes the absolute truth only comes out when someone is angry

Small-town politics cannot be taken personally

Quarrels would not last long if the fault were only on one side

A tremendous price is paid when there is hatred in the heart

Time heals all wounds

Get what you want, then enjoy it

Actions, not words

All your beginnings are important

All's well that ends well

Treat the world well

A good education makes a difference

Love things that are beautiful and think all things are beautiful

Good counselors lack no clients

One must be something in order to
do something

Be kind to animals

Success is action—a journey,
not a destination

Work expands to fill the time allotted
to it

There are no rules for love

If you play with matches, you will
get burned

There is no such thing as a free
lunch

Learn from adversity

There is no security on this earth;
there is only opportunity

Enjoy your wedding

Love the way you want to be loved

Don't be offended by the truth

In order to achieve a goal, one must
be set

Injure no man

Great minds think alike

It takes less time to do something
   right than to explain why you
   did it wrong

Hold your head up high

Action should culminate in wisdom

Love makes all things possible

Forgetting is a habit

Use common sense to rule your life

An injured friend is the bitterest
   of foes

Love in your heart eases pain caused
   by others

To understand the true character of
   a person, watch how she reacts
   in a time of trouble

Make decisions based on things you
   choose and not just alternatives

See clearly

Friendship with yourself is needed
   before you can be friends with
   anyone else

Laughter negates many insults

Live up to your potential

Shop in local stores

Hearts are meant to be broken

In relationships, the most important
thing is trust

Order needs flexibility

Good teachers make subjects
interesting

An idea can last longer than the
person who thought of it

Praise should make you a better
person, not an intolerable one

A minute of thought is worth more
than an hour of talk

Life should be a series of adventures

Understand what makes other
people tick

You don't have to be a comedian
to be funny

Live within your means

A hunch is creativity trying to tell
you something

Begin to live as you wish to live

Balancing work and leisure makes
them both more enjoyable

Every person must climb out of his
own hole

You cannot live on love alone

Beginnings are better than endings

Don't rush through life

Quit blaming everything on your
parents

Instead of thinking about doing
something, do something

Harm nobody

Words can heal and reconcile
relationships

Look at old problems in a new light

Tools and engines are only
extensions of man's limbs
and senses

If someone can do it, you can do it

Accept the worst

The more equal a relationship is,
the more natural it becomes

Look at everything in yourself as though in another person

Don't be critical of your spouse's friends

Life is too important not to be taken seriously

Necessity is risk-free

Measure life in experience not years

Find the place where you do your best thinking

Outrun destiny

Happiness is more than riches

Love the one you're with

If youth knew, it would take advantage of its age

Do not demand perfection in yourself or others

There is no such thing as too much common sense

Go for it

Be useful

Don't squander time

Your perspective depends upon your position

Act

Take advice from those you admire

Have faith in yourself and in your family and friends

Keep company with people who inspire you

Watch your language

If you want something done well, do it yourself

Be hearty in your approbation and lavish in your praise

Birds sing after a storm

Detours are opportunities to experience new things

Keep growing quietly

People who were happy as children tend to be happy as adults

Thought is free

It is better to give than to receive

We judge according to our own set of values

Relish small pleasures

A little nonsense now and then is
   pleasant

Always look for what others overlook

Summon your strength to get you
   through tough times

Examine what is said more than who
   said it

It is not enough just to exist;
   you have to live

Be faithful

If you greet a stranger, she usually
   greets you back

Master fear

Food tastes better when the table
   is well set

Fill your days with ambitious goals

Affirm your potential by realizing
   your individuality

Question your prejudices

Responsibility is the taker-away
   of youth

Time cools, time clarifies

Walking benefits both physical and mental health

To be interesting, be interested

If you could be well served, serve yourself

Have the strength to forgive all offenses willingly

Accept what you've asked for

Be careful with whom you compare yourself to

Doubt everything at least once

It is not what we do but how we do it that counts

When all else fails, read the instructions

Don't kill a fly with a hatchet

There is no accounting for taste

Don't count on luck

Be decided in what you will not do and you will be able to act on what you ought to do

You cannot make someone love you

If you are afraid to do something and
    do not do it, you lose out twice

Do not be afraid to work hard

As long as you are going to be
    thinking anyway—think big

The first to say "I am sorry" is
    the winner

Stop feeding your ego

Patience is the key to paradise

A wicked tongue is worse than
    an evil hand

Good education makes for a good
    future

If you think you can, you can; if you
    think you can't, you can't

Do not blow your stack

It is always darkest before dawn

The easiest way to learn something
    is to like it

Set aside some books you want
    to read

You are happy because you think you
    are happy

The grass is always greener on
the other side of the fence

The place to be happy is here

There is no excess in charity

Believe what you say

Treat your children like you wanted
your parents to treat you

Why love happens cannot be
explained

Reach for the high apples first; you
can get the low ones anytime

Rediscover your lover

Honesty pays

Trees bring places alive

Choose a profession for love, not just
for money

Not to advance is to recede

Good conversation should be
exhausting

Show respect for the other person's
opinions

The best ideas are the ones that
make the most people happy

We generally feel the way we want to
about life

Do not hold back on your visions

Leisure is not enjoyed unless it
is earned

You learn more by listening than
by talking

Silence is one of the hardest
arguments to refute

The best kind of peace is peace
of mind

Passion drives people to accomplish
great things

He that is full of himself is empty

Knock the chip off your neighbor's
shoulder by giving him a pat
on the back

Each kind attracts its own

See the obvious

Clearly define the person you want
to be

Don't live with the brakes on

Drink when you are thirsty

If your sole goal is to impress people, then you can never achieve true happiness

Never argue with a crazy person

Love makes the world go 'round

Substitute a walk for a nap

We belong to the land just as much as the land belongs to us

When you bring in something new, throw out something old

Each day holds possibilities for great discoveries and hidden joys

Pennywise, dollar-dumb

Loving does not require thought, only emotion

You cannot open a book without learning something

Making compromises is not losing

You cannot guarantee that something will not happen to you

You choose your life

Resist telling others how something should be done

Life is only boring to boring people

Some pursue happiness—others
    create it

Don't try to top others' stories

Looking down or looking up for
    too long can have undesirable
    consequences

Don't bite off more than you
    can chew

Our greatest songs are still unsung

An hour's industry will do more
    to produce cheerfulness than
    a month's moaning

Do all things graciously

Do more than is expected

Go confidently in the directions
    of your dreams

Seek solitude

Problem solving is
    a great skill

Saving ten dollars a week over
    your lifetime will add up to
    a lot of money

Knowledge will set you free

Creativity can solve almost any problem

Enjoy your success, but never quite believe it

Use, do not abuse

It is better to be lost with someone else

Worry is misuse of the imagination

Become a thoughtful person

Be who you want to be not what other people want you to be

There's no harm in asking

Mistakes are either cheap or costly, but there is always a price to pay

Wonder is the beginning of wisdom

Maturity is about experience, not age

The kite flies because of its tail

The future arrives every day

Don't be concerned with other people's impressions of you

He who saves another life adds years to his own

Nature's intentions are always about
preservation

The difference between stumbling
blocks and stepping-stones is the
way you use them

Take responsibility for plans that do
not succeed

A chip on the shoulder is a good
indication of wood higher up

Nothing brings more pain than too
much pleasure

Do not assume anything

See everything as though for
the first time

You can be any age and feel at peace

Slow and steady wins the race

Give all of your attention to the task
that you are doing

It is easier to fool yourself than to
fool others

Rats desert a sinking ship

A sense of humor is good to have at
any age

One man's loss is another man's gain

When something happens, the only thing in your power is your attitude toward it—you can either accept it or resent it

Integrity pushes you up to the next level of development

Be decisive

Pull your own weight

Keep your cool

Teach your kids to take responsibility for their actions

Develop a one-hundred-watt smile

Luck and strength go together

He bears misery best who hides it most

It is not what you know, but who you know

Nothing is so strong as gentleness; nothing is so gentle as real strength

No matter what happens in life, there can always be an occasional bright moment

By having fewer wants, you come
closer to knowing yourself

Save money

There is a lot of ground between one
extreme and another

Written words should be simple
yet effective

Laughter is good medication

It takes all sorts to make a world

Never trouble another for what you
can do for yourself

Live virtuously

Kids need more hugs than they need
things

Listen to your mother

Cherish your reason

What a day may bring a day may
take away

Go beyond your limitations

Some of the most wonderful things in
life are not meant to last forever

When life becomes too simple and easy, nervousness sets in very quickly

Make the grade

Stretch beyond what is comfortable

If you make people smile, they are more likely to do business with you

Adjust to the difficulties of life

Treat all equally

Do more, hope less

Give to yourself, so that you can really give to others

Going the extra mile puts you miles ahead of the competition

Do not make other people feel bad about your successes

Do things for the pure joy of it

Consider what comes first, then what follows, and then act

Since people have not changed in millennia, history should be our best teacher

The best cause requires a good
   pleader

Learn to wait and assess instead of
   acting on instinct

Education is essential to a well-run
   society

The worst part of success is trying
   to find someone who is happy
   for you

People need to control passions,
   not be controlled by them

Make your mind run your body

Delay is dangerous

Don't overestimate what money can
   do for you

Cherish your children for what they
   are, not for what you'd like them
   to be

A patch is better than a hole

Seize the day, put no trust in
   tomorrow (Horace)

The pen is mightier than the sword

Make investing a habit

Some defeats are only installments
   to victory

Do a good turn daily

Teach children to behave at home
   and they will know how to
   everywhere else

Remember special occasions

You cannot preach what you
   practice until you practice
   what you preach

When passion fades, replace it
   with compassion

Time even eases the pain of
   the young

By learning to obey, you will know
   how to command

Patience is the best way to
   accomplish things

The greatest of all riches is not
   desiring them

You cannot follow two paths

No one ever said it would be easy

Actions create heroism

Be happy with who you are and what
you have

Even the best writer has to erase

A promise is not as good as a deed

Leave the party on a high note

Everybody has something to lose

Learning is healthy

Open every door

Even if you're on the right track,
you'll get run over if you just
sit there

Every word has a meaning

Don't waste time grieving over past
mistakes

Know what you are doing

Do not rely on others for your
happiness

Remain rooted in your own purposes
and ideals

Pay what you owe

It is never too late to heal an injured
relationship

Be discriminating about what
images and ideas you permit
into your mind

It takes two to fight

Don't ask questions you don't want
answers to

The greater the obstacle, the more
glory in overcoming it

Well-known things are often not
totally understood

You must be aware of a loss in order
to lose something

Effort brings satisfaction

Nature is stronger than man

Diplomacy is thinking twice before
saying nothing

Keep an item of clothing seven years
and it will come back into style

Pretending to be in love will make
you less happy than not being
in love

Challenge yourself

Stand up and be counted

Do good deeds in order to benefit
    other people, not yourself

Do more, talk less

Fight for love

At work, if you watch the clock, you
    will always be one of the hands

Love is more valuable than money

A person never knows where his
    influence ends

Don't bite the hand that feeds you

Convert life into truth
    (Ralph Waldo Emerson)

Do not let part of you die while you
    are still alive

Don't compare siblings

The amount of happiness you
    achieve is determined by how
    much effort you put into
    achieving it

Stand by your friends in their hours
    of need

The optimist sees opportunity in
    every difficulty

Find employment where you want
to live

Grievances should be slept on before
being aired

Stick to your guns

Bad things can and do happen to
good people

A helping neighbor is better than
a helping government

How you say something may be more
important than what you say

Where the head goes, the feet will
also go

Believe in the good of people

Ask advice, but use your own
common sense

Remember your past achievements

Nothing very bad or very good ever
lasts too long

Avoid people who are negative

Respect children

You become older before you
realize it

Let the punishment fit the crime

A happy heart makes the face
cheerful

Have passion for one thing and
be interested in a thousand
other things

Thinking is the best medicine for
mind and body

Life goes on even if you are sick

Everything is caused

Try to understand the words that
you live by

Enter a room like you own the place

How children are treated
represents the success
of a society

What you can do is limited
only by what you can dream

A caress is better than a career

Be content with your lot

If you fuss over anything, you will
spoil it

There is even something good about
bad luck: it can change

Bait the hook well and the fish
will bite

Live each day doing for others
something that also enriches you

This too shall pass

Cultivate your talents

Friendships are made stronger
by time

Only say "I love you" when you
mean it

The majority is often wrong

If you want an easy job to seem hard,
keep putting off doing it

Be gentle

Self-preservation is the first law
of nature

The happiness of your life depends
on the quality of your thoughts

Don't bother closing the barn door
after the horse has run away

You can feel younger longer than you
are young

Let your play be exercise

Some fights are unavoidable

Gentleness often disarms the fierce and melts the stubborn

In the end, truth will conquer

Men of few words are the best men

Life should be an adventure

Do the research

Your efficiency depends on your ability to organize

Remembering happiness is like enjoying it twice

Initiative is doing the right thing without being told

Opinions have the right to be changed

We do not always gain by changing

Don't be astonished at anything that happens in life

Take time to watch the sunset

When you get older, all times are the good old times

Write letters to old friends

Most shortcuts are not shorter

If things stay the same, then there is no progress

Life is a mystery to be unraveled, not a problem to be solved

Explaining your intentions wastes everyone's time

The older the fiddle, the better the tune

Keep a stiff upper lip

Neither give nor take offense

A life in the service of others is worth living

Carry your part of the load

Make sure you understand your beliefs

Fight fairly

Think more about what you ought to be, not what you ought to do

Love is not measurable

Remember, even monkeys fall out of trees

You cannot bring back spoken words

Observe the speed limit

Always leave them wanting more

Don't accept "good enough"

No bird soars too high if he soars
    with his own wings

Wise people listen to those who
    oppose them

Wish upon a star

Help yourself first, then ask others
    to help you

Set both short- and long-term goals

If you live in the river, make friends
    with the crocodile

Treat your friend as one who may
    become your enemy, and your
    enemy as one who may someday
    be your friend

There is no boosting someone up
    a ladder unless she is willing
    to climb

Love beyond boundaries, beyond
    the physical, beyond the human

Be cheerful even if you don't feel
    like it

Black is black and white is white

Know when you reveal a weakness

Keep your promises

If you look at life as a bonus, then every day is filled with joy

The things most familiar to us are the things we most take for granted

Conduct has the loudest tongue

Stare truth in the face

An ending is better than a beginning when you create a piece of art

Live within your income

Take the time to recharge yourself

Kind words do as much good as mean words do harm

Sometimes it is wise to withdraw and regroup

You snooze, you lose

Take advantage of an advantage

Outlive your enemies

Some events are more fun when you go with a group of people

Better late than never

The key to communication is precise
definition

Poetry is so inspiring because so
much is said from so little

You have enough

Being quiet does not always mean
you have nothing to say

Envy accomplishes nothing

It is never too early to begin
investing for your retirement

Peers have a bigger effect on
children than parents

Whining does not solve problems

No man is better than he wants to be

Support family businesses

If you want to change something,
convince enough people that
it needs to be changed, then
change it

No person can climb beyond the
limitations of his own character

Awareness adds to life

A coach feels a loss more than the players; the players feel a win more than the coach

Try to keep bad situations from getting worse

Doing is better than saying

Go where there is no path and leave a trail

Do the right thing at the right time

Curl up with a good book

Believe and conquer

Work diligently

Good times are better when remembered with friends

Periodically change your look

Evil to him who evil thinks

You're not responsible for what others think of you

If you command wisely, you are willingly obeyed

A guilty conscience needs to confess

The reward of a thing well done
is to have done it
(Ralph Waldo Emerson)

People are in such a hurry to get to
the "good life" that they often
rush right past it

Stolen hours are the sweetest

You are your own example

A work of art can be perfect but filled
with imperfections

Do not overuse the word *no*

If the counsel is good, take it

If you enjoy your life, your children
will enjoy theirs

Take a leap of faith

Hold your child's hand every chance
you get

Remember how short time is

You cannot argue with success

It is more difficult to show
moderation when you are in the
midst of prosperity than when
you are not

Do not hinder important business for
the discussion of a trifle

Enthusiasm is a learned skill

The early bird catches the worm

Look back and see how far you
have come

Being too sane is a sign of madness

The person who does not know
himself is a poor judge of
other people

Nothing is as powerful as the
moment a person learns
something new

After the feast comes the reckoning

Let your heart inspire your life

There will always be new challenges
ahead of you

Intuition is often as important as
the facts

Enemies keep you on your toes

It never hurts to be polite

Defeat educates us

The worst kind of enemy is one who
used to be a friend

Visualize your goals

You can never go wrong when you
follow your dreams

Make the best and wisest use
of your time

Success has a lot to do with attitude

Enthusiasm is a driving force that
overcomes all obstacles

Simplify your life to achieve balance

What the superior man seeks is
in himself (Confucius)

Love is a more natural feeling
than hate

You can learn something from
anyone

Learn to spell

Create and maintain a peaceful
home

The best tranquilizer is a clear
conscience

Be original—even eccentric

Do not believe things that are
not true

Be innovative

Nothing in the world can take the
place of persistence

A good example is the best sermon

To know the road ahead, ask those
coming back

There is always room for discovery

Chasing wealth isn't a way to
be content

A busy mind breeds no evil

Making love has a learning curve

Delusions help make life worth living

Living successfully means pursuing
your goals

Your will is always within
your power

Humor is the best icebreaker

Remember your past mistakes just
long enough to profit by them

Find more time for yourself

It is more costly to blow a second
chance than a first one

Learn to cope with rejection

Surround yourself with talented
people

Your head must take your heart into
consideration when making
decisions

A good laugh and a long sleep are
the best cures

Concentrate on the present

Use your vacation time

The best investment for income
is honesty

Love yourself first and everything
else falls into line

Call things by their right names

Overtip waiters and waitresses

Do not quit trying during trying
times

No one can tell you who you are

You can say anything you need to say
if it is done in kindness

Life is 10 percent what you make it
and 90 percent how you take it

Do not tell all of your jokes at
one time

Circumstances do not make a person,
they reveal a person's character

Remedy your imperfections

Changing what you do will change
how you think and feel

Be modest

Make sense of your world

Don't underestimate your power
to change yourself

Slow down your responses

Ask for what you want

Keep your private thoughts private

The more adventures one goes on
in life, the more stories one has
to tell

Order and method make things easy

The biggest human temptation
is to settle for too little
(Thomas Merton)

Truth is the truth no matter what
others may think

When you are in love, it shows

A bad marriage is worse than no
marriage

There is still an old-fashioned way
to do most things

Thank your children's teachers

Better to be happy than wise

Say what you mean

He who cheats another cheats
himself most

Sweet are the uses of adversity

How a person acts is a true test of
his character

Get organized

Use your head and heart together

Strike while the iron is hot

Don't antagonize people

Cut the coat according to the cloth

Death does not know prejudice

Only you can put your ideas
into action

Everything is possible if you want
    it badly enough

Friendship should not occur at
    a price

We are smarter than we know

Do not find fault with what you do
    not understand

Stand out from the crowd

The trick is to live a long time
    without growing old

Do not fly your kite too high

Experience must be understood
    for it to be an experience

Prevention is the best cure

If you think you are having a good
    time, then you are

Trying harder to accomplish things
    makes you feel better

People take you at your word

Show your love to win love

Empty what's full

Keep your good deeds silent

The only things left after you die
  are the good deeds that you
  performed

The truth is relative

The imminence of death should make
  you live

Never mention the worst—drop it
  from your consciousness

The best way to understand nature
  is through observation

Be led by reason

Be patient to listen to someone's
  entire thought

Tact is making a point without
  making an enemy

Beauty is universal

Drink enough, but never too much

A friend in need is a friend indeed

Talents need exercise

You never really lose until you
  quit trying

Keep your cool, no matter how dire
  the situation

All you need to have fun is one good friend

Playing is a child's work

It is easy to lose weight; keeping it off is the hard part

A perfect traveler creates the country where he travels

Look forward to better days ahead

Meet others halfway

Move forward in the direction of your convictions

It is better to be looked over than overlooked

An hour wasted can never be regained

Your actions define you better than anything else

One cannot feel happiness all of the time

Enjoy a moment of solitude

Learn how to think clearly

Forgive yourself

To make the cart go, you must grease
the wheels

Energize yourself

Behave like a free spirit in the
presence of fate

Get to know your neighbors

Money isn't everything

Even logic has its limits

Nature is a work of art in progress

Happiness is found in the small and
simple things that happen in life

An original is always better than
a copy

We cannot always oblige, but we can
always speak obligingly

You can tell more about a person
by what he says about others
than you can by what others
say about him

Everybody is unique in his own way

Don't attend the auction if you don't
have money

The best way to turn people off is to
continually talk about yourself

He who knows no laziness will know prosperity

Size doesn't mean much

Love is a cure for loneliness

Think before you speak

Dig deeply

Recognize when you see something good

In order to feel good remember what it is like to feel bad

Become addicted to good and healthy ways

Live so that your children know you are fair, caring, and full of integrity

In the pool where you least expect it, there will be fish

The good and the bad that you do in your lifetime lingers on after you have left

Adventure is all about personal discovery

Possibilities are infinite

A great part of the information you have acquired was gotten by looking something up and finding something else on the way

Ask for support

Anything is possible

Wherever you are right now has the potential to be paradise

Be a player, not a spectator

Practice your passion

What is worth doing at all is worth doing well

Imperfections make life exciting

Try to smile when everything goes wrong

Reading a book is like living another life

It is never cheap to get sick

See more than what your eyes show you

Never lose the desire to play

It is easier to give advice to other people than to yourself

The mind should change with
conditions

If it isn't one thing, it's another

The more things change, the more
they remain the same

Listen to your children

When in doubt, do nothing

Happiness is what you make of it

Take every opportunity to do
better work

It is often the last key in the bunch
that opens the lock

Don't worry about things outside
your control

Discovery gives life its meaning

The best way to walk through life is
with integrity

Seek new pleasures

Do not kiss and tell

It is never too late to learn
new things

Retirement should be the frosting on
the cake of life

Expect nothing

Your community is the world

Time works wonders

It is better to be what you are than
    to struggle to be what you are not

Man does not live by bread alone

Everything must wait its turn

Give credit where credit is due

Enjoy the good times in life because
    the roof can cave in at any time

The amount of happiness
    experienced depends on what
    comes from within

You can be much more influential
    if people are not aware of your
    influence

Remember the nice things that
    happen to you

Do not spend too much of your time
    earning a living

Tap into the positive universal
    energy that exists in life

Art makes a good teacher

Accept life's limits and inevitabilities and work with them rather than fight them

Practice asking for help

A broken heart brings on the most wisdom

Have confidence in your abilities

It is better to have an aim and miss it than to not have an aim

Happiness is up to YOU

Do something nice for someone else—and don't tell anyone about it

No situation is so bad that losing your temper will not make it worse

Doubts need not be hidden

Wake up and become aware

Quitters never win, winners never quit

Never lie, cheat, or steal

Be exact

Enemies must agree on peace for it to last

You cannot always have things
exactly as you wish

Of two evils, choose the lesser

The proof of the pudding is in
the eating

Enjoy a good laugh when it is apt

Working to improve yourself is more
difficult than wanting to improve
yourself

A person can never have enough
hope

Guilt can be an overwhelming
emotion

Society succeeds when it is easy for
people to do good deeds

A great idea can affect eternity

A lie can never be true

The man is richest whose
pleasures are cheapest
(Henry David Thoreau)

Believe in dreams

The catching ends the pleasures of
the chase (Abraham Lincoln)

Be quick to praise people

Nothing is more injurious than
unoccupied time

Bad drivers should not have
good cars

Kiss and make up

A nickname lasts forever

Love makes all burdens light

Savor each day

Put the important people in your
life first

Never think that you're not
good enough

Let yourself go

Keep the agreements you've made

Do not speak ill of the dead

Nip the problem in the bud

It takes a lot of work to make a
house a home

Find joy in what you have

Every situation and every moment is
of infinite value

If you don't use it, you lose it

Show enthusiasm in both work and
    leisure

You do not have to give up having
    fun just because you are an adult

Be humble

Don't be a cynic

Dare to stretch your giving to
    new levels

Good health requires that you
    have your body, mind, and
    soul balanced

To err is human

Use your twenty-four hours in a day

It is skill, not strength, that
    commands a ship

He who looks behind will never
    get ahead

When in doubt, mumble

Make big plans for yourself

We never repent of having eaten
    too little

Once something is said, it is hard to
    take it back

Dump your unwanted baggage

Responsibility begins in dreams

Each moment is too precious
to waste

Spoil your partner, not your children

Cooking is art and science combined

It is not only what we give but how
we give it that counts

Have realistic expectations

The right thing to say is usually
thought of too late

Train yourself to have better habits

When you get to the top, the climb
just begins

Discover hidden passions

The artist is the most individual

If you are determined to not fail at
a task, then you will not

Live all you can; it's a mistake not to

Wisdom takes years to acquire

He who wishes to rest when he
gets old ought to work while
he is young

Experience the mysterious

A single idea acted upon can change
humankind

Let go of the what-ifs

Choice is the difference
between good and bad

Happy is the person with
a hobby

Without health, no one is rich

Patience is the companion of wisdom

Seek to understand

To the victor go the spoils

Do not sell yourself short

Nothing worth having can be
purchased

It is natural that a liberal youth
will eventually turn into a
conservative adult

Go after a great job because you can
always get a job you do not like

Success is about making
opportunities for yourself

Do not ask for trouble

Cherish leisure because it is a rare
    commodity

Do not let yourself become insulated
    from life

Love is a constantly growing
    experience

Good conversation consists of talking
    about everything and nothing
    at all

Being totally alone, at times, can be
    very healthy

Laugh and the world laughs with
    you; cry and you cry alone

Just because you are not as good as
    others does not mean you should
    give up

Find your own philosophy

Even if you do something ridiculous,
    outrageous, or stupid, do it with
    enthusiasm

There is no such thing as a perpetual
    enemy

Do not let the sun go down on
    a quarrel

Don't accept unacceptable behavior

Honor what is honorable

Let others have the glory

The outside world needs to be in
　　your realm of self-concern

To be good is easy; to be great
　　is difficult

People act the way times dictate

Common sense goes a long way

There are tricks to every trade

Force is no argument

To live a full life, you cannot live it
　　half dead

Resolve to live each day by the
　　Golden Rule

Life is short enough without violence
　　and war making it shorter

Do not think there are no crocodiles
　　because the water is calm

You can be happy if you want to be

There is no one true definition for
　　the word *retirement*

You can guilt yourself into a
   miserable life

Give with joy and joy is your reward

Creativity is in our genes

Reward yourself with things that
   make it worth it for you to go on

People know more that is false than
   is true

Faith is working in the dark

Discouragement promotes inaction
   and inaction guarantees failure

Be master of your will and a slave to
   your conscience

Music is good for you whether you
   are happy or sad

It is easy to perform an act of
   goodness; but it is difficult to
   keep your mouth quiet about it

You cannot buy class

Inner direction gives strength

Our prime purpose in this life is to
   help others

Diminish your demands, especially
   on others

Remember that children do not think like adults

Advances in life are usually first met by fear and skepticism

Read for ideas

You can feel lonely even if you are not alone

Try anything once

Greatness is only achieved with the help of passion

Better to limp along the right road than to speed on the wrong one

There's a simple philosophy to saving money: keep more than you spend

Others never appear as complex as us

A big head means a big headache

If you want peace, stop fighting

Let your imagination make a nice life for you

No one is altogether good or altogether bad

Better ask twice than lose your
way once

Good health is priceless

Most of today's problems will have
solutions one hundred years
from now

Experience is lived, not created

People treat you the way you allow
them to treat you

Survive failure

Friendships are bound by common
interests

Allow for unstructured time

Create an unhurried morning
routine

It is better to have income
than to be fascinating

One great golf shot wipes out
a hundred bad ones

No luxury should be purchased
with debt

If you try to sit on two chairs, you
will sit on the floor

Everybody has a bad day once in
a while

Music can have a tremendous effect
on the emotions

Do not sacrifice your principles to
please anyone

Everything put together falls apart
sooner or later

Your right to vote is a great equalizer

Dare to go beyond your comfort zone

Comparisons are unfair

No man ever got lost on a straight
road

Follow nature

A genius is more than just
intelligent—she is applying that
intelligence to do good

Fools outnumber wise people

Every person has a fatal flaw

In order to have a meaningful life,
one must experience adversity

Them that has, gets

Two people look at the same thing
and see totally different things

Love is blind

By endurance you gain rewards and
comfort for your pains

Knowledge does not have a ceiling

There is no substitute for good
manners

The laughter of children makes
a home

Double-check information gathered
on the Internet

The philosophers of the world have
said everything important that
needs to be said

Be happy when other people succeed

Exceed your goals

You'll never know how strong you are
until you get tested

Love is an energy booster

We must not give up, even when we
think no change has taken place
in our character

Never do by force that which may be done by fair means

Try to progress—that's a big part of progress

You cannot fake integrity

Think otherwise

Look up, laugh loud, keep the color in your cheek and fire in your eye

Don't deceive yourself

Both of your feet must be on the ground before you can jump in the air

The optimist sees the doughnut, the pessimist sees the hole

Having an education is different from using an education

Find a way to do what you love

Investing in love returns priceless interest

People who laugh a lot make more sense out of life

Computerize your grocery list

Read directions carefully

It is easier to catch up on work than
it is on fun

Be careful about the company
you keep

The active soul is the one thing of
value in the world

God is in the details

Pass along your best

The more hands, the lighter
the work

Know on which side your bread
is buttered

Search for hidden opportunity
in events

Aim at fulfilling whatever talents
you have inherited

Feelings need expression

There are two kinds of people:
the people who lift and
the people who lean

Gardening can be more than
a hobby; it can be a passion

Every train has a caboose

History is full of dead people

Don't try to live forever; you will not
    succeed

Too much knowledge is just as bad as
    not enough knowledge

Generalizations are seldom true

Sometimes doing nothing is
    the best thing to do

Thinking is a state of mind

If opportunity knocks, let her in

To be happy when things are not
    going well is courageous

Politeness is inward kindness
    outwardly expressed

Sometimes it is smart to not show
    your success

Concentrate on what is right in front
    of you

Await occasions, hurry never

Good communities offer a sense
    a belonging

The better lived, the shorter life feels

He labors in vain who tries to please
    everybody

Talk less and say more

Avoid quarrels

Live so that value is added to
your life

A lifetime of opinions makes a person
look like a hypocrite

A comfortable bed can make the
coldest days seem warm

Strengthen yourself with
contentment

When you are afraid to do
something, do it anyway

Flirtation is meant for the young

Keep your sense of humor

Energy and persistence conquer
all things

Money cannot buy you youth

When you are upset, tired, or
stressed, stay away from
the fridge!

Know when enough is enough

It should not be in a child's power to
cause you any disturbance

Enjoy what you have attained in life

Put yourself in others' shoes and
take the focus off yourself

Do not advertise what you cannot
fulfill

Be content to seem what you
really are

Enjoy each age of your life

An ideal listener will have enough
compassion to honor our feelings

A nail can go no farther than its
head will let it

The best way out of a difficulty is
through it

The less we know, the more we
suspect

Don't listen to those who say you're
taking too big a chance

To do good is to be good

Expect adversity

Love wisdom and live according to
its dictates

Paper is patience: you can put
anything on it

Love needs to exist for life to go on

Listen to experience

Getting on is partly a matter of
    getting up each time you are
    knocked down

Live life on high energy

Put your feet on your own
    coffee table

In an argument, first try to see
    the other's point of view

Anger comes from being hurt

Simplify your eating habits

Freedom knows no fear

A person's greatest emotional need
    is to feel appreciated

Keep your watch set a little fast

A lie is like a snowball: the farther
    you roll it, the bigger it becomes

Leave no stone unturned

Words are the most powerful weapon
    in the world

You can run, but you cannot hide

Imitation is highest form of flattery

Don't say, "You shouldn't have"

People judge you by the friends you keep and the enemies you make

Never leave hold of what you've got until you've got hold of something

Grandparents' advice can come in handy

Short time here, long time gone

Personal growth requires reflection

Begin your dreams

Life is so interesting because it is imperfect

Try never to think negative thoughts about yourself

You get out of the world just what you put into it

Search for the good life

It is easier to talk about other people than about politics

Observe nature working

Every artist was first an amateur

Take care of the possible and trust God with the impossible

Combat things within your power that are not good for you

When you love someone, you get to live two lives

Cultivate compassion

Don't flaunt your success, but don't apologize for it either

Petty cares wear the soul out drop by drop

Laughter does not spoil the skin

Fear less, hope more

Birthdays are good for you

Creative thinking is inspired by limited funds

Don't let go of your values

No one goes through life without suffering

Changing your mind always has impact

Do not eat your pies before they are made

A good deed is never lost

Think about the best thing that
happened today

No two people remember the same
event exactly the same way

Seek friendships

Marrying for money is the hardest
way to earn it

Fearing death accomplished nothing

There is a difference between the
way things are and the way
things should be

As we are inwardly, so shall we
appear outwardly

Dare to ask outrageous questions

The more known, the greater
the judgment

The ideal is truth at a distance

No one knows the weight of
another's burden

When you are in a hole, stop digging

It is better to light a candle than
to curse the darkness
(Eleanor Roosevelt)

Always think about things—as they are, not as they are said to be

Hunches are usually based on facts filed just below the conscious level

Nature, to be commanded, must be obeyed

Your work should enrich your spirit

Love is part of nature

The problem about a good thing is that if you tell too many people about it, it ceases to be a good thing

People often condemn others for what they see no wrong in doing themselves

A good scare is worth more than good advice

Become centered in the flow of your life

The grass may be greener on the other side, but it still has to be mowed

Take short views, hope for the best, and trust in God

Tell people only what needs to be
done, not how

You are part of a big world and
an even bigger universe

You may regret what you say, but
never what you do not say

Difficulty strengthens the mind as
labor does the body

Laughter and crying sound the same
in all languages

A journey begins with a single
step, and a road map

All cats look alike in the dark

Don't weigh yourself every day

Good posture means better health

A drop of ink may make a million
think

Remind friends of their own worth

Life has a certain responsibility code

There are some qualities in life that
cease to exist once we realize
they are happening

Learn to let go

Be prepared for difficult times

Envy can consume the envious

Love is more understanding with age

Let go of the disappointments and pains of the past

The wisdom of life consists in the elimination of nonessentials

Love can make the wisest look foolish

All that glitters is not gold

Persistence will accomplish more than force

Do not give too many of your secrets away

A rolling stone gathers no moss

Tap into your special talents

You only feel old if you have nothing to do

The sun shines after every storm

Art should effect your mood

Wish to know all the truths

There is more joy in anticipation than in realization

What we learn early we remember
late

An apprentice becomes an expert by
and by

A child's expectations of her life are
more important than your
expectations for her life

Great art is difficult to explain,
but easy to see

Love for your children should never
have conditions

The titles of some books are better
than the actual books

People can change, so give them
the benefit of the doubt

Seeing someone succeed is an
opportunity to learn new methods
for your own success

Such is the state of life that none are
happy but by the anticipation of
change

Meet your losses with gains

The truth is always believed
eventually

Greed never has an end

There is no greater crime than loss of time

The secret of science is to ask the right question

Perfect practice makes perfect

When things look blackest, happiness is often just around the corner

Treat a highly intelligent man like a highly intelligent man

Good thoughts are half of health

Blaming others is silly

Write down your fears to make them separate from you

Don't be too critical of others

The two H's: health and happiness

Once you are inspired by knowledge, nothing looks or feels the same again

A person's value depends on his ability to stick to a thing till he gets there

No plans should be small

Maintain the utmost respect for
human life

Be your own reliance

Notice your feelings; let them flow

Understanding what is in our control
and what is not in our control
is an important element of
a happy life

Prefer stimulating talk versus trivial
chatter

Praise twice as much as you criticize

Everyone has pluses and minuses

In all things do your best

Good bargains empty your pockets

You can't sell the cow and have the
milk, too

Control your habits, do not let them
control you

Put some color in your cheeks

Spend time with clever people

Like breeds like

Living itself is an art

Many friendships begin after a bottle
of wine is shared

Honor is the throne of integrity

Each sorrow has its purpose

The voyage of discovery consists
in having new eyes

You need energy and spirit to
overcome life's obstacles

Meet your deadlines

You can't believe everything you hear

Don't lose sight of the future

Praise others in public

Ability is of little account without
opportunity

Forgiving benefits both the one who
is forgiven and the one who
forgives

Contribute something to your culture

Not everyone recovers from a tragedy
in the same amount of time

Time is not for sale

Find the things you want to do

Enjoy the earth

Become compassionate

You cannot live on promises

What you must do, do cheerfully

Age does not have to be the brake
of life

If you cannot help, do not hinder

Establish a pace in life

A believing love will relieve us of
a vast load of care

Lower your tolerance to stress

Do not cry so hard about your hard
luck that you cannot hear
opportunity knocking

Find pleasure in being creative

It makes little difference what is on
the outside of your head if there
is something on the inside

Old is fifteen years older than you

Timing is everything

Hold yourself accountable for the
way you feel

Be a friend to yourself and others
will soon be

Be courteous to older people

Do not try to control everything

Hasty climbers have sudden falls

Doing should be more important
than receiving recognition

Love what is inside you

Having passion toward something
makes the unimaginable
imaginable

Fair words butter no parsnips

Plan things out in your imagination

It is tiresome trying to please all
people

Little things worry little minds

Success, for the most part, makes
people humble, tolerant, and kind

It does not matter so much where
you live as how you live there

Experience is the best teacher

Have more money by having fewer
wants

For everything you have missed,
    you have gained something else;
    for everything you gain, you lose
    something

Be in agreement with nature

Never marry someone in hopes that
    he'll change

Forgive like you want to be forgiven

Politeness is to do and say the
    kindest things in the kindest way

Look for inspiration

Let your children do things their way
    if no great harm will result

You can bring a horse to water,
    but you cannot make him drink

Your dreams are more valuable than
    money

Don't worry, be happy

There is so much imitation in life
    because imitating is easy to do

Heroes just go further than ordinary
    people

Good examples are easy to follow

Marriage is an art

Prosperity comes from spending money wisely

No person knows a lot compared to the realm of all things

Take advantage of the little opportunities and you will not need to wait for the big one

Don't try to run anyone else's life

All good things must come to an end

The fiddle is judged by its tune

One man's food may be another man's poison

Let go of anger; it hurts you more than the person you are angry at

You are only young once

Wit should amuse, not abuse

Compliment even small improvements

Enjoy each stage of your child's life

If you can't stand the heat, get out of the kitchen

It is more difficult to help others when you are feeling low than when you are feeling up

You can patiently hope

Soul mates are forever

Study hard, think quietly, talk gently

As you walk, look for miracles
   along the way

Happiness is a by-product
   of an effort to make
   someone else happy

A marriage bound by beauty only
   lasts as long as the beauty

Surround yourself with bright,
   cheerful colors to lift your spirits

To understand life, one must live it

Make only agreements you plan
   to keep

Today is not any other day

The greater the hurry, the worse
   the speed

Love removes hate

Don't send a boy to do a man's work

Believe in unlimited potential

Learning how to breathe properly
is the most important exercise
technique to learn

The less you watch television,
the less you need it

The idea that something is just
around the corner gives radiance
to everything

Begin at the beginning

Maintain self-respect in the face of
a devastating experience

A glorious moment can live in your
head a lifetime

As much time should be spent
exercising the mind as is spent
exercising the body

Never feel guilty when you are
caring for yourself

The only way to be found is to first
become lost

Simple things are beautiful

Bad beginnings can turn into
good endings

The best bridge between hope and despair is often a good night's sleep

Try hard not to make the same mistake twice

Happy people love life most of the time

Comfortable fashion lasts the longest

Give peace a chance

Wait for the right moment to act

Ask and you shall receive

Failure is not an option

Buy at least two of anything you use a lot

Consider yourself with more respect

Be or pretend to be brave

Remind yourself that when you die, your "in basket" won't be empty

Try to love all of the seasons of the year equally

Your dreams are achievable

Laughter is a brush that sweeps away the cobwebs of the heart

Decisions are easy when you know
where you are going

Don't cut corners

Never mistake motion for action

When something becomes clear,
act on it

Adults are nothing more than
children with obligations and
responsibilities

If you sleep with a dog, you will rise
full of fleas

A little dirt never hurt anyone

Materialism is addicting

Irony makes life worth living

Be the person you thought you would
become

Create what you are looking for

Drinking when you are happy is
better than drinking when you
are sad

The wise learn from history

A clear conscience is a coat of armor

Count on being alive tomorrow

An idea can always be improved

When you feel love, you are more
connected to the universe

A person must lose innocence in
order to gain knowledge

Care enough to listen

Have a desire to improve things

From a broken violin, do not expect
fine music

Expect grave consequences if
nature's laws are broken

Life is meant for the living

You can spend a lifetime searching
for the meaning of life

If you want a characteristic, act as if
you already have it

Just because something is not
familiar to you does not mean
it does not exist

The truth frightens many people

Opposing sides can still cooperate
with each other

Anything accomplished with passion
is enjoyed

The best teachers make the best
  pupils

People who put off little things
  never get big things done

Keep your overhead low

Make a difference in life

Do something every day that you
  don't want to do

When you really think about it,
  truly think hard about it—life
  is strange

If you try to kill time, it will
  eventually kill you

Unchecked speech is like
  a vehicle out of control

Better little joys than big
  disappointments

The future should always appear
  rosier than the past

Search for the secret of tranquility

The shadow of generosity is broad

Life's dividends depend on interest

Failure is less of a crime than low
  ambition

Force yourself to be active

Money begets money

Don't just stand there, do something

Ideas are the mind's medicine

Since you cannot make more time,
spend the time that you have
more wisely

Reason is the lamp of the mind

A beautiful face or body only lasts for
so long

Be master of your thoughts

You can't expect to hit the jackpot
if you don't put a few nickels in
the machine

Laziness does not breed success

Love freedom

It is easy to endure the misfortune
of others

Good company can meet anywhere
and it will be good company

Do everything; one thing may turn
out right

Lies are usually told to make
something appear better than
it is

Be better to your neighbors and you
will have better neighbors

The wise do not need the things
the unwise crave

You can never do a kindness too soon

What cannot be cured must be
endured

A remark generally hurts in
proportion to its truth

Play more than spectate

Think yourself happy

Know that you have lived well by
facing your final end with joy
and peace

You must be able to forgive yourself
before others can forgive you

Let other people think what they will
think

Character should be valued

Be on your guard against a false
sense of self-importance

Compliment people every day

It is better to love someone you cannot have than to be with someone you cannot love

It can be wise sometimes to conceal your abilities

Spend valuable time getting ahead, not getting even

People are the same all over the world

Cheerfulness keeps up a kind of daylight in the mind

The man who has a right to boast doesn't have to

Don't look for trouble

Don't try to keep up with the Joneses

Forgive those who hurt you

Never think that you have done your fair share of good

It is good to have many options available in an uncertain environment

The hand that gives, gathers

Transform negatives

Be more comfortable doing rather than being

Great people say great things

If you aim at nothing, you usually get it

Change your toothbrush every three months

Different jokes for different folks

Have weekend retreats at home

By justifying things, you can make the worst appear better

Do not think you are the only pebble on the beach

Do not expect money to bring you happiness

Opportunities make equality

Try a thing three times: once to get over the fear, twice to learn how to do it, the third time to decide if you like it or not

The more you love someone, the easier it is to forgive him

Get it in writing

Stand your ground

Love is impossible without understanding

You cannot conceal your true character forever

Love can make you do things you would normally never do

A closed mouth catches no flies

Do not cross the bridge till you come to it

A good friendship makes both people happy

Know both sides of the case before you open your mouth

Liars have lots of practice

We learn by mistakes

The door to success is labeled "push"

In death, everyone is equal

Believe that you can learn anything you need to know

Danger attracts more than safety

You have to crawl before you can walk

Focus on making things better

Live a life so that when you die more people are sad than happy

The best way to get the last word is to apologize

Make the other person feel important—and do it sincerely

Sometimes when you lose you still win in the long run

The best friends are those who have the same ailments

Find out all you can in life

When you accept death, you can begin to truly live

In every affair, consider what precedes and what follows and then undertake it

Destiny is not a matter of chance; it is a matter of choice

Envy is the enemy of happiness

Your real enemy is within you

Talk less, say more

Keep your nose to yourself and it will not get cut off

Look forward to your next adventure

The best revenge is to live long enough to be a problem to your children

Play your cards right

Man is made by little things

Efficiency is getting the job done right and effectiveness is getting the right job done

Confirm all appointments

Do not feel like a fraud

You do not need freedom in order to be free

Smart people have an insatiable thirst for knowledge

To live our dreams, we must wake up

Be a good loser and a good winner

Be sure you are right, then proceed

Life is all about the unknown

If you try to please everyone, nothing gets done

Patience cures everything

Failures can be an installment for later successes

You are never too wise to learn

If you can read, you can live as many
lives as you wish

A marriage can never be judged from
the outside

Every day begins with the unknown

Give simple gifts

Enjoy a little and endure much

It is good for your body and mind
to age at the same rate

Remember people's birthdays

Share your sorrow with
a friend

Many things are easy to learn, hard
to master

It takes a wise person to recognize
another wise person

Age is no excuse for foolishness

Ignorance is dangerous

Be careful of anyone who does not
have a sense of humor

Do something with the rest of
your life

A person ought to do what she thinks is right

Poverty consists in feeling poor

Knowledge thrives on gaining knowledge

Drive your business or it will drive you

To avoid risks, stay in bed

One man does not make a team

Repair the roof when the sun is shining

The world does not stop for a broken heart

Most yes/no questions are answered no

Work hard at your marriage

Wisdom is all about learning how to live a better life

Seek the truth

A reunion is living history

Have enough reasons for wanting to stay healthy

He who is in the mud loves to pull others in

Friends are chosen, not relatives

Strengthen the body

Insist on yourself; never imitate

A part of kindness consists in loving people more than they deserve

Understand your actions

A clear conscience is often the sign of a bad memory

Opportunities look for you when you are worth finding

Most people are what they should be

Don't let pursuit of your dream hurt anybody

Do not say that you do not have enough time

A leopard cannot change his spots

Having experience in accepting ourselves, we can extend compassion and tolerance to others

Fruits and vegetables taste better when you pick them yourself

Everyone who is not in love wishes
that he were

Invest in your talents and beliefs

Stop trying to do it all

The world needs leaders and
followers

Heaven is a place prepared for those
prepared for it

Replace smoke detector batteries
every January 1

You can gain knowledge from
everyone

What you do not know cannot
hurt you

Organization requires order

Put first things first

A bath can be a mini-vacation

Your friend is your needs answered

A journal is an interior journey

Hide nothing from your minister,
physician, and lawyer

Focus on people's positives

The fish is soon caught who nibbles
at every bait

The dinner table is a great place
to learn

Believe in the equality of man

To govern a child is to govern
yourself first

Think big, but let the little things
make you happy

Pride costs us more than hunger,
thirst, and cold

Treat all religious matters reverently

Lessons hard to learn are sweet
to know

Every action has an opposite and
equal reaction

Satire is both amusing and
instructional

Find love within yourself

Death sharpens our appreciation of
what it means to be alive

Make the best of your situation

Adults treat children according to
how they act

Many of life's lessons involve some
form of pain

You usually end up where you are
supposed to

Learning is addicting

Every human being has some handle
by which he may be lifted

The way to love anything is to
realize that it may be lost

Resign from any organization whose
meetings you dread

No one is wise enough by himself

Love accepted is twice as strong as
love given

Please all and you will please none

Lots of what you do does not show,
like the roots of a tree

Dig the well before you are thirsty

Happiness has two enemies:
pain and boredom

Love begins life

Dance to a different drummer

Watch your back

Know the true value of time

Compromising is the easiest way to
  end an argument

Recognize mere appearances for
  what they are

Have a steady diet of good literature

Advise upon what you have
  experienced

He who is his own friend is a friend
  to all men (Seneca)

Don't tell tales of yourself to your
  own disadvantage

Life is more pleasurable when lived
  according to nature

Always make a good entrance
  and exit

Don't be the first to break a family
  tradition

Be yourself

Do your homework

Do what you have to

Laugh and be well

The shortest way to anywhere is to
have good company with you

Don't wear a hat that has more
character than you do

The lead sled dog has the best view

Be able to be alone

A problem, when solved, is simple

Learn what you do not know

Show enthusiasm in gratitude and
appreciation

No one knows what will happen to
him during the day

Everybody could be wrong about
what is right for you

The more down-to-earth you are,
the more relaxed you become

Let the light of your heart show you
the direction to go

The mind must first be blank in
order to learn

You can ruin the present by worrying
about the future

Say a lot in few words

It is when you give of yourself that
you truly give

All animals are equal, but some
animals are more equal than
others

If you do not look for imperfections,
you will not see them

The more you know, the less
you enjoy

Anger is a great motivator

Study meditation

A good offense is the best defense

Miracles occur in gardens

Hope for the best, but prepare for
the worst

A stumble may prevent a fall

The guide of life is common sense

Get happy

Give more than you planned to

A generous action is its own reward

Talent first, confidence second

Choose a self and stand by it

Even laughter should be taken
seriously

Make the atmosphere of your life
more pleasant

Eventually the right solution will
appear

Good things can be painful

Alter the difficulties or alter yourself
to meet them

You cannot get something for nothing

Wisdom is a paradox: it teaches us to
have no limitations, but it also
teaches us to be aware of the
ones we have

Do not put your life on hold

Don't worship the god of other
people's opinion

Schedule time for your inner work

A good library takes learning
seriously

Soften your most stubborn positions

Most people don't realize that both
help and harm come from within
ourselves

Sometimes free advice is worth more
than paid advice

Notice opportunities

Be slow to forget what you have
learned

You don't need to be the class clown

Rediscover some of the mysteries
of life

To love is a stronger feeling than to
be loved

A day is filled with many moments

Every life has interesting facets

Each stage of life has a learning
curve

Always have some project under way

Listen to yourself

Interest and attention will ensure
your education

Art creates balance

Faithfulness is the antidote to
bitterness and confusion

Money and class do not go hand
in hand

Go through life with a dreamer's
  attitude

The unexpected always happens

The road is all

Play close to the chest

Love can be felt by everyone

Use your energy positively

The most wasted of all days is the
  day when we have not laughed

No amount of special effects can
  make a poorly written movie into
  a good movie

Make haste slowly

A healthy marriage puts the
  marriage before the children

He who has money receives more

The only normal people are the ones
  you do not know very well

Any place you hang your hat is home

As man thinketh, so he is

If you have nothing to do, at least do
  it with other people

The material needs to come before
the work

Every life has its own riddle

Advice is usually not free

What the eyes see at an early age
influence the brain through
old age

Eat your vegetables

The human race has survived despite
itself

Every age has its superstitions

If you can make someone laugh, you
can do just about anything to her

A great library is the diary of the
human race

He was a bold man who first ate
an oyster

A fool cannot take a joke, so jest with
your equals

Be busy in the present lest you be
caught unprepared in the future

The bigger they come, the harder
they fall

Balance requires you to manage
in the short term as well as
the long term

The things that torment you most
are the very things that connect
you with all the people who are
alive or who have ever been alive

Hear twice before you speak once

It is better to be good than lucky

Read, study, and learn about
everything important in your life

Do creative work before chores

A verbal contract is not worth the
paper it is written on

Money cannot buy happiness

Your hand is never the worse for
doing your own work

Rise earlier than others for more
peace and a sense of personal
fulfillment

Two heads are better than one

Question everything

Learning to laugh at yourself is
the surest sign of maturity

A wallet is empty until it is filled
with pictures

True knowledge comes from
experience

Unhappiness creates more
unhappiness

If you want to make a parent proud,
compliment his child

Vow to speak purely and lovingly

The present is for action

Outward beauty is not enough

Never take advice from someone who
is in worse shape than you are

Never underestimate the power of
forgiveness

Want what you can have

Meditation is the art of being at one
with yourself

Only you know if you are winning
the race

Not every cloud is a sign of a storm

Nature's rules are reasonable

Do not dismiss something as useless
just because it is not understood

A great idea can give your life
direction and purpose

Regret nothing

A headline does not necessarily tell
the story

If you curse others, you will
be cursed

Believers in life and the bounty of
life find their coffers are never
empty

Silence is golden

Men's natures are alike; it is their
habits that carry them apart
(Confucius)

Do not sign up for things you hate
to do

Find pleasure in the task

We become in part what our senses
take in

You cannot shake hands with
a clenched fist

Never alienate anyone on purpose

You can conquer if you believe
you can

Keep lists of important things

Recognize the important everyday
accomplishments of your life

Be gentle with the earth

Happiness need not be analyzed

Money can be very sexy

Life is a struggle that must
be accepted

Don't drink and drive

Choose where you want to live and
then look for work; not the other
way around

The wisest people know how to love

You usually do not know that you
are in a bad mood until someone
brings it to your attention

A minute lost in the morning is
never regained all day

In relationships, the differences are
opportunities to enrich our lives

Only a foolish person never feels
hurt

Get involved at your kid's school

A committee of one gets things done

The same thing happened today that happened yesterday, only to different people

Retirement means many different things

Today is the first day of the rest of your life (Albert Hoffman)

Sometimes the smaller problems are more difficult to solve than the big ones

It is easier to educate the mind than the heart

Much truth is spoken in jest

Freedom isn't the right or ability to do whatever you please

Age is the great equalizer

Trust your hopes, not your fears

Too many commanders cause confusion in the ranks

This is a good time if we know what to do with it

Keep your ancestors alive in your heart

Vulnerability is often the price of growth

Give sail to ability

Children follow examples, not advice

Achieve happiness

Play to win

Some things are better forgotten

Life should be lived with a certain pride

Share your wealth

Be superior to your possessions

Prepare yourself for reality

Succeed at integrating work and play

Be objective even when deeply attached

Something is learned every time a book is opened

Take as few things personally as you can

Allow a walk to empty your mind

Decision making takes practice

Nature is experienced through *all* the senses

If you know how to live well, a lifetime is enough

Toothaches never get better on their own

Judge a person by his deeds, not by his words

Be yourself before being someone else

Remember kind things that have been done for you

All things are possible

It is easy to let your desires rule you

Share happiness

When one evil comes, a million follow it

Frivolous talk is hurtful talk

Paint what's in your head and what you're acquainted with

The brook would lose its song if you removed the rocks

When speaking in public, know your audience

Love what you do

Hit the books

The bad workman blames his tools

Places can give inspiration

A pet has just as much fun being
played with as you have playing
with it

Progress comes from people who
are not satisfied with the way
things are

The fellow who blows his horn the
loudest is likely in the biggest fog

Stay interested in life

It is a lot easier to react than
to think

Knowledge is a responsibility for
the integrity of what we are

Never be fully satisfied with your
work

Pessimism is more harmful than
optimism is helpful

Lift yourself up by your own
bootstraps

The best kind of pride is pride in
your work

Even if you win an argument with
a child, you really did not win

Respect the opinions of the old

Parenting is a practice

Send the right signals out

Happiness as well as sadness comes
and goes

Take the first step of the journey of
a thousand miles

Know your limitations

A man's word should be as good as
his bond

Remain on life's sunnier side

The hope of reward sweetens labor

Knowledge of others' failures is
a timesaving strategy

Get the money honestly

Enjoy your efforts

Most people do not become what they
thought they would become

Let your reason be supreme

The more you reveal, the safer
you feel

He profits most who serves best

Consider carefully your natural bent
for a business or a profession

A good teacher gives more than
the students can handle

No one is skilled in everything

It takes very little effort to become
outstanding

Think hard before you burden
a friend with a secret

A wise person knows how to forgive

A man is known by the promises
he keeps

Life is not a popularity contest

No one can be happy 100 percent of
the time

There is not half the pleasure in
possessing an object as in the
effort to attain it

Tell the truth and expect the truth

Live it up

Knowledge comes by trial and error

Know when you see quality

Merit wins

There are no secrets to success,
only hard work

Economy is the art of making
the most of life

A moral inventory does not mean
that we condemn ourselves

To lengthen your life, lessen your
meals

When you are surrounded by beauty,
you look at life differently

They that have patience may
accomplish anything

Mind reading is only for mind
readers

In a friendship, because you share,
the good times are double and the
bad times are cut in half

Integrate what you believe in every
area of you life

There is no good and evil in nature

You've won the game if your children
still like you when they get older

When an argument flares up,
the wise man quenches it
with silence

No time like the present

Having strong principles can be
costly

Attention is to people what fertilizer
is to flowers

Let your hook always be cast

If you cannot join them, start your
own league

Be someone you would want to be
friends with

The wisest mind has something yet
to learn

Understand yourself in order to
understand others

Don't be afraid to stick your neck out

Want more than you can see

If you worry, worry with someone
else

There is only one part of your
    life that you cannot change:
    your past

Don't hide when you fail

Dealing with difficulties prepares
    you for life

He who makes us do what we can is
    a friend

Do not lose courage in considering
    your own imperfections

People make the town

When you do not know where you
    are going, any road will get
    you there

After three days, fish and guests
    stink

Use the old before getting new

The two hardest things to handle in
    life are failure and success

Keep your chin up

Energy creates energy

Everyone has demons to overcome

Let your heart fill with wonder

Either lead, follow, or get out of the way

Do not be afraid to do something badly

When love stops growing it dies

What your life turns out to be is usually different from what you thought it would be

Never give up on anybody

Do not feel shame at being helped

Expanding the mind creates the most happiness

It does not matter that we will not attain a state of perfection or complete humility in our lifetime

You must not expect old heads upon young shoulders

Get the butterflies in your stomach to fly in formation

Love is a great beautifier

There was never a good war or a bad peace (Benjamin Franklin)

Do not speak ill of yourself; others will do it for you

Discover your skills

Don't tell jokes that can hurt
someone else

No one but yourself can be blamed
for the loss of your soul

Nature is a giant canvas and life is
the artwork on it

Judge not, lest ye be judged

The greatest good you can do for
another is to reveal to someone
her own riches

Words often do worse than blows

Slow and steady wins the race

It is never foolish to forgive

Two people loving equally is a rare
occurrence

Reflecting will teach you patience

Hate is usually caused by fear

Truth is more important than
consistency

Most great ideas are usually first
misunderstood

Diplomacy is the art of letting someone else have your way

Some decisions need to be made from the heart instead of the head

Always strike a fair deal

It is better to be in the position of giver rather than receiver

Your mirror will tell you what none of your friends will

Have a purpose for everything you undertake

Prolonged bad weather can negatively affect even the happiest person

Discover the essential things that are missing from your life

Every stage of life has its pluses and minuses

Examine your life

Return all phone calls within a day

Every man must bear the consequences of his own actions

Even the darkest cloud has a silver lining

Elbow grease gives the best polish

Be a good listener

Your daily life is your temple and
your religion

A common cover-up for hurt is anger

There should be nothing you should
not want to know

Never trade your tomorrows for
a yesterday

Never interrupt when you are being
flattered

If you look the part, you'd better be
the part

Embrace your failings

Rain makes the flowers grow

The willingness to do creates
the ability to do

It is more fun to work for a company
that is growing than for one that
is dying

Pause for enlightenment

Do not change the rules in the
middle of the game

Good ideas are born in minds that keep working

If it sounds too good to be true, then it probably is

Feel the passion within, not for possessions outside

The only thing a heated argument ever produced is coolness

Always in a hurry, always behind

Only the mediocre are always at their best

Learn as you'd live forever

We see things more than just with our eyes

Talking is one of the fine arts

Ride over all obstacles and win the race

No matter how hard you try or how much time you spend worrying, some things just cannot be changed

A good marriage gets better with time

Laugh at death

Through our collective experience, we have found that we can accomplish together what we cannot do alone

Beware of people who seek power

Know first who you are and what you are capable of

To fill the hour—that is happiness

You are free when you tell yourself you are free

Choose the lesser of two evils

As long as you are alive, you can still hope

Kindness is a great peacemaker

Events can only change your life if you let them

Do what you love

Know what you like

A good liar easily recognizes another liar

Don't dig your grave with your knife and fork

God hides things by putting them near us (Ralph Waldo Emerson)

Knowledge begins with awareness
of self

To know when you have enough is to
be rich

Life shrinks or expands in proportion
to one's courage

Be happy with the life you create

Wait and hope

Time spent with your children is
not wasted

Sleep when you are tired

If you've lost your sense of humor,
find it fast!

Anyone who dares to waste one hour
of life has not discovered the
value of life

Search out the cause of things

What goes around, comes around

All men are brothers

Children should do their share of
household chores

You always win when you compete
against yourself

You are only a victim if you allow
    yourself to be

Think of ways to improve your life

Measure twice because you can only
    cut once

Your first thought should be good,
    but your second should be better

Grudge not another what you cannot
    attain yourself

It is easier to be a politician than
    a scholar

Be prepared to lose once in a while

The power to choose is yours

Forget what you know in order to
    learn new things

Vigilantly practice indifference
    to external conditions

The brain interprets what
    the eyes see

Great teachers can open up the
    world to students

If it is a big party, you can consider
    buying a new outfit

The older one gets, the more careful
he becomes

Love your job

Rule lust, temper the tongue, and
bridle the belly

Failure is essential to learning

It is always best to start at the
beginning

Don't let what happened yesterday
inhibit what is happening today
or tomorrow

Avoid losing your temper

Amid all your duties, keep some
hours to yourself

Be the first to reach out or act loving

Worrying about dieting excessively is
not healthy

When you start thinking you are
having a good time, the good
time is usually over

You must bring the artist into
the world yourself

Every garden will have a few weeds

In a good marriage, both people usually keep their mouths shut half of the time they want to speak

Willpower is guided by self-discipline

You possess inner beauty longer than physical beauty

Try to always head in the right direction

Life should not be a spectator sport

You find most things when you cease to look for them

Don't sell yourself short

Work hard at finding great pleasure in the simple things in life

All fires start out small

Good health begins in the mind

Every life has a story

Discipline for children needs to be fair and spoken softly

When you have reached the mountaintop, then you begin to climb

All advantages have their price

Life teaches us the same lesson over and over again until we learn it

Get justly, use soberly, distribute cheerfully, and live contentedly

As he thinketh in his heart, so is he (Proverbs 23:7)

A field becomes exhausted by constant tillage

Business is business

Life contradicts itself

Education is the ability to listen to almost anything without losing your temper or your self-confidence

Don't smoke anything

All the negatives of politics do not even come close to outweighing the few positives

Hope springs eternal

Discover the work you love

You never know how much you enjoy doing something until you try it

Do not insult the mother alligator until you have crossed the river

An hour is an hour for everyone

You cannot please everybody

Don't tell people what you're going to do, let them wonder about it

Your work is on your work

What pains us trains us

Don't discuss domestic problems with friends or at work

You can sleep when you are dead

It is how you play the game that matters

Do not judge your neighbor unless you are in his situation

Don't live life so you die disappointed

If your mind becomes thirsty, then drink wisdom and knowledge

Foresight is better than hindsight

Enhance the confidence of others

People who know how to act are never preachers

Learn from the world

Do boldly what you do at all

Review your life regularly

A cloth is stronger than the threads
    from which it is made

Liberty is the power to do things

Expect the unexpected

Love passionately

A true friend never gets in your way
    unless you are going down

Listen to the patient

Real progress occurs when the young
    feel it is time to change things

Never answer a hypothetical
    question

Talk turkey

We meet all life's greatest tests alone

Only death can save you from
    old age

Bury the hatchet

Beauty comes from the soul

Great pains cause us to forget
    the small ones

No challenge is ever easy

Never take away hope from another

Make your boss look good

Enjoy humor

Live and learn

Cherish the circle of people that you
have in your life

Don't overdo it

You can learn more from people who
disagree with you than from
those who agree with you

You do not need to buy a cow just
because you like milk

It is always more fun to watch big
sporting events with other people

Figure out the criteria with which to
measure your life

Fame is better than fortune

Pray for your enemies

A good education will never decay

The answer depends on the question

Though the ant works its heart out,
it can never make honey

The closest we come to death when
we are living is when we have
no opinions

Hold to your purpose

Facts do not cease to exist because
they are ignored

Try not to use time or words
carelessly, as neither can be
retrieved

You can never arrive at your final
destination without taking
a first step

Don't follow the advice of a fool

Pay no attention to things that don't
concern you

Be determined to live a happy life

The good life is the life of inner
serenity

You have an obligation to be
an individual

Sometimes it feels like the world has
forgotten you

Caring makes the world a better
place

Really look at the landscape

It is more important to understand
the piece of art than the artist

Keep your capacity for faith and
belief

No bird soars too high, if he
soars with his own wings
(William Blake)

The shortest distance between two
points is a straight line

It is not things that disturb us,
but our interpretation of their
significance

A life not lived is lost

Do not put self-imposed limitations
on yourself

Sometimes it is better to say
something different than what
you are thinking

Self-help is the best help

Drink because you want to not
because you have to

Find a job from which you never
want to retire

Life is a balance of holding on and
letting go

You hit only what you aim at

You become addicted to adversity
before you become bored with it

Feel whole

When you have nothing to say,
say nothing

Energizing requires movement and
oxygen

Common goals make good friends

There is safety in numbers

Don't choose a profession just for
money

Nothing in life is accomplished
without hard work

Know when to stop worrying and
move on to something else

Be careful what you say

Someone has to win the lottery

Everything can be experienced

A struggle always precedes progress

Keep on trying until you get it right

If you look at life as an adventure,
then it will be

Don't spread yourself too thin

The most important thing in any relationship is not what you get but what you give

As the twig is bent, the tree's inclined

No matter how thin you slice it there are always two sides

Problems don't get better on their own

Don't take action when you are angry

You are the painter and life is your canvas

Accelerate your efforts

Singing cures sorrow

You don't get something for nothing

Work is the best way to kill time

Enrich time shared with friends by being attentive and open

Make it happen

Look forward to the beauty of the next moment

Let kids win when you play games with them

Resolve to be the master of your destiny

Feed your passions

God finds a way for what none foresaw (Euripides)

If you cannot run with the dogs, stay under the porch

Go ahead and change whatever displeases you

Don't wait to start improving the world

The more you live, the more you see; the more you see, the more you know

Learn from past mistakes and move on

A man is what he believes

A sense of community is good for the soul

Medicines were not meant to live on

Life was created with room to grow

Know a hawk from a handsaw

The love of change is as natural to man as it is to nature

Good ideas live forever

Don't make the sauce till you have
caught the fish

Accept yourself like you accept
others

Being a grandparent is your reward
for being a parent

Only he who attempts the ridiculous
can achieve the impossible

Be kind to yourself

We are shaped and fashioned by
what we love

Education is what makes people
different

Thinking about money all the time
takes away precious time for
thinking about other things

Turn over a new leaf

Be slow to judge others

A little dirt never hurt anyone

Be tired at the end of every day from
doing a lot

Opportunity seldom knocks twice

He who accepts nothing has nothing
to return

Figure out what you are going
to do tomorrow

Happiness sneaks in through a door
you didn't know you left open

Every possession implies a duty

Pleasures should not cause pains

Art gives life meaning

Contentment causes the greatest
happiness

Sit still in the boat that
carries you across
deep water

Children never really lose an
argument with their parents

Sparkling eyes are not just for
the young

Education is never a waste of time

Listening matters

Look out and not in

May you be alive when you are alive

Doing is different from saying

Without inner peace, it is impossible
 to have world peace (Dalai Lama)

Mistakes turn into experience

Fix the mind first and the body
 second

Never assume

Bear, do not blame, what cannot
 be changed

In every job, the beginning is the
 most important part

Liberty is one thing you cannot have
 unless you give it to others

Happiness makes health; health
 makes more happiness

Everything can be looked at from
 a different view

If you have to do an errand, make it
 two so it's worth going out

Love comes in all sizes, shapes,
 and colors

If it is going to come out eventually,
 better have it come out
 immediately

The things we worry about tend not to happen

Pleasures should not be attained guiltily

The future comes one day at a time

By knowing what you can and cannot do, you will get more done

Write your diary in secret code

Hobbies take time and energy to flourish

An afternoon in the garden is better than one with a therapist

One of the greatest pleasures in life is the discovery of something new

A good mate is hard to find

Building on good fortune is like building on sand

The more you eat, the more you want

Successful marriages have times of solitude

Feel free to experiment with new ideas

Love conquers all things

You talk when you cease to be at
   peace with your thoughts

What a difference a day makes

Assume all is well—yet not perfectly
   secure

Many drops of water make an ocean

Be a happy person

A kind word goes a long way

Character is higher than intellect

Old friends are the best friends

Endure patiently that which cannot
   be avoided

There are no easy answers to unclear
   questions, questions not properly
   asked, and stupid questions

Buy only properly fitting shoes

Music is a great bridge

Authentic happiness is always
   independent of external
   conditions

Live life so that your descendants
   will think you did good

Breathe before you speak

Keep love in your heart

"I can't" means "I won't"

The love of truth and excellence have
power to save you

Law was made for man

Common opinions spur friendships

Take action when you need to

The wise man keeps his own counsel

Don't count on miracles

If you put nothing in your head, you
will get nothing from it

To see takes time

Having money does not guarantee
a happy life

Do not let another's opinion sway
your judgment

Offer something to the world

Only through trial and suffering is
the soul strengthened

Stay loose

Nothing tastes as good as vegetables
from the garden

Make others feel appreciated

There is no one right way to be
   a parent

Do not drown yourself to save
   a drowning man

Plan big

Timing is everything

Happiness is measured by one's
   experience with feelings of
   happiness

Let the buoyancy of beginning carry
   you to new places

Much profit, much risk

Truth will out

One friendship can change your
   world and how you feel about life
   and yourself

Death can show us how to live,
   can teach us about life

You cannot keep a good man down

Constant occupation prevents
   temptation

Freedom lies in being bold

It is easy to err in telling the truth

Look for opportunities to make people feel important

Be genuinely interested in other people

What you do not want others to do to you, do not do to others

Repeat directions back to the person who gives them to you

Time makes us different people

Tell the truth or someone will tell it for you

Everyone can be changed by an event

Pain is easier to handle when you go through it with another person

Everyone is naked under their clothes

Keep a pad and pencil in every room

Expect nothing and you will not be disappointed

We are all inventors

Do not take down a fence unless you are sure why it was put up

We all share the same earth

Keep company with those who may make you better

A learned person is twice born

Be careful not to claim victory prematurely

Beware of making final, irrevocable decisions in a hurry

It is in his own interest that the cat purrs

Do not change horses in midstream

If you would be loved, love and be lovable

A good neighbor smiles at you over the fence but does not climb it

A ruffled mind makes a restless pillow

A light heart lives long

Do not shoot the messenger

Always be ready to follow a new lead and shift techniques

Do not rain on anyone's parade

Life is shorter than we think

Nothing endures but change

In conversation, ask questions more
   often than you express opinions

It is exhausting to be insincere

Learning refines and elevates
   the mind

Disappointments and unhappiness
   arise from our false notions of
   things and persons

He judges best who thinks least

There is nothing we cannot live
   down, rise above, and overcome

Not all paths are clear

Don't betray any confidences

Be happy with the parents you have,
   not the ones you wish you had

Little said is easily amended

It does not cost anything to say nice
   things

A deep person believes in miracles

Keep in perspective the value of
   money

Believe that life is worth living
   and your belief will help create
   the fact

Humiliation is felt when a job is lost

Learn to live in the present moment

Make the most of every sense

The best morsels are never given to a beggar

Nature stands waiting to be enjoyed

If you crave a rich food, eat a tiny portion

The problem with stretching the truth is that it's liable to snap back

The little things in life determine the big things

Affection is the broadest base of a good life

Get even with the people who have helped you

When in doubt, tell the truth

Take the money and run

Happiness is contagious

Do not let what other people might think affect your behavior

Invention is the natural outcome
of creative thinking

Listen when spoken to

Date for fun, marry for life

He who blows in the fire must
expects sparks in his eyes

Dead people have no faults

Keep moving in the direction of
your goals

The proper use of imagination is
to give beauty to the world

Know when to ask for help

Rejoice in each day that fortune
grants

Experience is a good teacher

Never delight in another's
misfortune

The most important thing parents
can teach their children is how
to get along without them

Learn how to manage your parents

In the midst of tragedy, remain calm

Stop aspiring to be anyone other
than your own best self

Each day, set aside some time
for a little fun

Every day is a lifetime

Sometimes a mosaic is as
beautiful as an unbroken
pattern

Think things through and then
fully commit

To be conscious that you are ignorant
is a great step to knowledge
(Benjamin Disraeli)

Adversity is a great teacher

The half hour a day you spend
exercising more than doubles
in return

Don't let anyone intimidate you

Don't compromise yourself; you're
all you've got

If you don't throw it, they can't hit it

As you think, so you become

With age comes certain privileges

The cat in gloves catches no mice

Love of the game is more important
than winning

Pay as you go

Never change a winning game

He who knows himself is enlightened
(Lao-tzu)

Cleanliness is next to godliness

Happiness does not have to feel
foreign to you

Assert yourself

Nothing is ever as good as you think
it is going to be

Life teaches us to be less harsh with
ourselves and with others

Don't be unwilling to learn

Every man is the architect of his
own fate

When you're angry, count to ten

Listen to your brain

Take the bad with the good

Death is the greatest mystery

A person cannot be totally happy or
totally sad

Save for a rainy day

Do not interfere with your ability
to see answers

It is better to suffer an injury than
to inflict one

When a marriage works, nothing on
earth can take its place

Material things never make a person
happy for an extended period of
time

It isn't the whistle that pulls
the train

Shout for joy

Know your facts

The business of life is not business
but living

Practice empathy

When trying something new, it is
better to do it badly than not do
it at all

Life is a promise to fulfill

It is not always good to utter one's
inmost thoughts

Giving something back to society can make you feel better

Never give up on what you really want to do

If you seek well, you will find

Become a better person from your trials and tribulations

Cheerfulness is the principal ingredient in health

Almost everything in life is easier to get into than out of

Resisting is easier at the beginning than in the middle or end

Decide what is important in life and disregard the rest

If you do not feel old, then you are not

The more attention we focus on our spiritual nature, the more it will unfold in our lives

Long faces make short lives

A trifle consoles us because a trifle upsets us

The human will can be strengthened like a muscle

A good host will spill the first drink

Be careful what you pretend to be

Do not protect yourself by a fence, but rather by friends

Cowards die many times before their deaths

Every man for himself

One small act of generosity can work wonders

A wealthy person is one who enjoys each day

There is only one way to enter this world, but many ways to exit it

A thing easy to get is easy to lose

No answer is also an answer

Take advantage of your gifts

Stare misfortune down with hopeful eyes

Be studious in your profession, and you will be learned

Don't bother remembering anything easily looked up

Silence is sometimes the best answer

Never treat a triviality as if it were a disaster

Create an awareness of what's going on in your life today

To be independent when you don't have money—that's the test

People can produce happiness for other people

Time will tell if true love exists

All of life's difficult questions usually have simple answers

A little wine inspires, a lot of wine numbs

It is easier to behave your way into a new way of thinking than to think your way into a new way of behaving

The way you take care of yourself in your forties affects how you feel in your sixties and seventies

Mistakes create experience

In union there is strength

Humble hearts have humble desires

Little things added up become big things

Life isn't fair

Remember the value of time

Do it now

If you haven't used it in a year or more, get rid of it

The good befriend themselves

A drastic lifestyle change can be shocking

Know when to stop

Never give up control of your life

Notice life's small joys

Eat and drink with your friends; do business with strangers

Happiness is a result of doing

Stop buying more stuff

Ignore those who try to discourage you

Keep on truckin'

Mistakes show us what we need
to learn

Grass does not grow on a busy street

Say, "Enough about me; I want to
learn about you"

It is harder to stand up against a
crowd than to go along with it

State your needs

Persevere

Don't make eating an issue with
children

Pay well for good service

If you must fail, fail with dignity

Refute without argument

No one has everything

Say thank you when complimented

Time is the most valuable thing one
can spend

The more the merrier

Battle prejudice and discrimination

There comes a time in everyone's life
when they realize that they have
to live with themselves

Moderation is the key to life

Envy lasts longer than happiness

It is just as expensive to purchase
    an old house and fix it up as
    it is to buy a new house

"Mistake" is food for a new invention

Nature cares nothing about money

Do not be a slave to your past

Treat other people as individuals

Friendship is a two-way street

You must constantly readjust to your
    surroundings

Think faster than you act

Acquire impeccable manners

Make sure your dreams are set high

Try to gain opportunities to hear
    wise men and women talk

Most people would rather get than
    give affection

Appreciate the times you are happy

Faith can never fully overcome doubt

Do what you do carefully

Taking a step back from a problem may give you the distance you need in order to see a solution

Do what you can

If someone throws you a ball, you don't have to catch it

Everyone is good at at least one thing

Desire is broken down into two categories: ones that we need and ones that we think we need

A good life does not mean an easy life

We speak as we tend to understand things

You will always fall short of perfection

If nothing else in life gives you pleasure, at least have good dreams

Never worry about yesterday or tomorrow

Very few opinions are written in stone

Conduct yourself in all matters in accordance with the laws of nature

Hope for your friends' successes

Intolerance is the child of ignorance

Success is defined differently from wealth

Once you know the facts, you can make intelligent decisions

Stress is always with us

Feather by feather the goose is plucked

Your journey will take you somewhere

Give credit where credit is due

Accept triumph and defeat with equal grace

One pound of learning requires ten pounds of common sense to use it

Take the stairs

Don't be swept off your feet by the vividness of the impression

Don't let them push your buttons

The sky is the same color wherever you go

Let love and faithfulness never leave you; write them on the tablet of your heart

It is possible to fall madly in love with just one glance

Never imitate

Things come back to you when you give to others

You can only lose what you have

Being truly sorry is a clear indication that your self-centeredness has diminished

Choose being kind over being right

Relax

Find your niche in life

Do not delay what your heart says

Never doubt an opinion made from the heart

Silly question, silly answer

Wisdom is a mixture of reality, dreams, and humor

Do three things for yourself each day

If you want to go to parties, you have to give some parties

Reminiscence never leads to anything new

Life is too short to be little

If you look hard enough, you can find a positive in any situation

The smartest people may ask a foolish question now and then

If you want to enjoy success, fantasize about it

Happiness shared with another person is twice as good

It doesn't hurt to be optimistic

Make nature a part of your life

You will never be asked to bear more than you can cope with

A man cannot leave his wisdom or his experience to his heirs

Be a friend to have a friend

Never give in

The dictionary is the only place
where success comes before work

Wisdom never ages

Men and women are different but
equal

Anyone can hold the helm when
the sea is calm

Some people need more than others

Blushing is the color of virtue

A wise person knows when
a shortcut takes less time

Try to work in an office with
windows

It doesn't cost anything to be nice

Feeling obligated to do something
can take all the fun out of
doing it

Know when to refuse something that
won't get you anywhere

Chance acquaintances are sometimes
the most memorable

Each life has its moments of truth

Seek the mysteries of life

Don't say, "I know how you feel"

Where there is cheese, there are mice

Actions alone do not make
a person good

Haste makes waste

Fear is a powerful emotion

It is easy to see happiness in other
people

Life is about taking leaps

The truth often hurts

A still tongue keeps a wise head

Difficulties are tools used to prepare
us for better things

Putting up with yourself can either
be a punishment or reward

Put some things on the back burner

Believing in yourself is the first step
to improving yourself

Do not criticize your neighbor until
you have walked a mile in his
shoes

Imagination creates art

Enthusiasm begins all great things

Feeling beautiful is more important
than being beautiful

Fight the good fight

Prefer enduring satisfaction to
immediate gratification

Mistakes are the portals of discovery

The accomplice is as bad as the thief

There are no unimportant acts of
kindness

No matter what you accomplish
or how far you go in life, you are
still you

Hold onto the railing when walking
down the steps

Rule your mind or it will rule you

Fractures well cured make us
stronger

Read the instructions

Set reasonable bedtimes for yourself
as well as your kids

Pay attention to everything with
equal force

You can learn a great deal from
an opponent

Clothes do not make the man

The pleasure of laziness is quickly
 replaced by the uncomfortable
 feeling of guilt

Each living being is idiosyncratic

Pleasures can be planned

Seek refinement rather than fashion

In order to be forgiven, one must
 learn how to forgive

Tentative efforts lead to tentative
 outcomes

If you can do something now,
 do it now

Love is not merely saying, it is doing

It is natural to want what you
 cannot get

Speak clearly and with grace

Spend some time each day acting
 like a child

Things done cannot be undone

Strip time of its illusions; find the
 quality of the moment

A goal can be met in more than one way

Insensibility is the companion of drunkenness

Keep some important personal things private

You build most of the traps that get you

Inactivity breeds ignorance

If you ask someone to do something for you, let her do it her way

Never give way to melancholy

Children and grandparents are natural allies

A sound mind and strong body come in handy in this world

We achieve by pursuing

The secret of the enjoyment of pleasure is to know when to stop

The memory of the past is usually better than the actual past

Love what a person is made up of along with the person

The more you love, the more you love life

Wisdom should be shared

Seize from every moment its unique novelty

Discover your own specialty

If A equals success, then the formula is A = XYZ. X is work, Y is play, Z is keep your mouth shut (Albert Einstein)

Never lose your soul

Carry your light with you wherever you are

Schools have one purpose: to teach students how to become self-educated

Charity of soul is greater than charity of money

Much knowledge is gained by listening

Do not put the cart before the horse

Two people can look at one thing and have different opinions

It is easier to learn something right
the first time than to have to
relearn it

Wonder

Control your thoughts

Write down mistakes so they are not
forgotten

Humor is the spice of life

Life is not so short but that there is
always time for courtesy

Leaders begin wars, not the masses

New ideas bring you to new places

Whenever you fall, pick something up

To do nothing is to be nothing

Do not make complaining a full-time
job

A question can be better than
an answer

Words are the most powerful drug
used by mankind

Begin in time to finish without hurry

Success arrives by not failing

Pick battles big enough to matter,
   small enough to win

Selfishness makes people predictable

Humility brings us back down to
   earth and plants our feet firmly
   on the ground

Trust your own judgment

Stop trying to control the
   uncontrollable

Our duty is to aid those to whom we
   think we can be the most useful

Laughing at the wrong time is still
   good for you

Ignore years and they will ignore you

No two people think alike

Have nothing in your house that
   you do not know to be useful
   or believe to be beautiful
   (William Morris)

Old age is for the strong

It is okay to change your mind

Love who you are

Life's crossroads do not have
   signposts

We learn from life

Life has a certain humor that surrounds it

It is better to enjoy others than to need them

Learn how to stand on your own

Trouble begins when more is said than necessary

Wisdom is the fruit of experience

You cannot have an adventurous life without taking chances

Everyday life is life

The trick is to have more good days than bad ones

Reacquaint yourself with old friends

Wise people know when and what to overlook

The journey is the reward

The mind must be free for limitless imagination

Those who search for the defects of others do not know their own defects

Love can never be hidden for too long

It takes many years to learn how to
   live life

Say no politely and quickly

Many philosophies can be true

Education pays for itself

The responsibility for your actions
   is yours

Using force only gives you
   a temporary advantage

Better to make a mistake than to
   do nothing for fear of making
   a mistake

Look for the extraordinary in
   the ordinary

Next to knowing when to seize an
   opportunity, the most important
   thing to know is when to forego
   an advantage

Keeping a secret is a difficult thing
   to do

Turn off the TV

Early to bed and early to rise makes
   a man healthy, wealthy, and wise

When you see something that needs doing, do it

It is good to know much but better to have use of what we know

Think a hopeful thought every day

With each passing year of your life, become a wiser person

Live consciously

There is nothing you cannot teach yourself by reading

Buy flowers that make you gasp

Learning has a snowball effect

Get in shape and stay there

A contented mind is priceless

Children should be taught ethics by example

Achieve flow

Making to-do lists is helpful

When you are outside of your comfort zone, rely on your intuition to take over

Everyone must learn by experience

It's easy to repeat; hard to originate

Sour, sweet, bitter, pungent—all
must be tasted

Bad deeds weigh more than good
deeds

Prioritize before you start work

Kiss slowly

Call a friend today

See problems as opportunities for
growth and self-mastery

Set aside time each day to be with
yourself

Ask, what is the right thing to
do now?

Kind hearts are gardens, kind
thoughts are roots, kind words
are flowers, kind deeds are fruits

When you are well, you want the
world; when you are sick, you
will give the world to feel well

Become at least half of what you
meant to be

Plan to have fun

Exchanging compliments is
intellectual back-scratching

When we honestly admit our wrongs, we find humility

The more a person talks, the less he actually says

Even a monkey will fall from a tree sometimes

Stop being a slave to your appointment book

Every day we are offered twice as many opportunities as misfortunes

Remind yourself to laugh and smile

Anticipation is an excuse for not enjoying the present

Music makes life more pleasant

Do not carry a joke too far

Good manners must be defined in order to be used

You do not have to be a coward to want peace

When we cannot act as we wish, we must act as we can

It does not make sense to worry
about things that can and cannot
be changed

Every man to his own opinion

The lowest ebb marks the turn of
the tide

Become adventurous in spirit

Assume that everything that
happens to you does so for
some good

Everything you think affects your
spirit, your mood, and your
ability to contribute to others

Question authority

The last lap is the hardest

Young people should make more
mistakes than older people

The members of loving families
would be friends with each other
even if they were not family

With no winter the spring would not
be so pleasant

It takes years to achieve self-
confidence

Everyone goes through trials in life
to get where they are

Always put off till tomorrow what
you shouldn't do at all

Better a lie that soothes than a truth
that hurts

Look out for the minutes and the
hours will look out for themselves

When a storm surrounds you,
remain calm

Sometimes people just need a hand
to hold and a heart to understand

Travel through life with a rich soul

Let all your belongings have their
places

Life goes in cycles between
happiness and sadness

Miracles do happen

Make sure the prize you chase is
worth the effort

Balance life's serious side with
its fun side

Thank someone each day

Determine what is essential in life

A quality life is more valuable than
a quantity life

Running errands can be
a full-time job

Give clothes you don't wear
to charity

Half the joy of achievement is
anticipation

Let your friends have their
peculiarities

Inspired people inspire people

Invent a celebration ritual with
a friend

The better you are, the more people
you influence

Politicians are supposed to serve the
people, not the other way around

Don't let yourself be rushed on
an important decision

Taste the joy that springs from labor

Youth is the caretaker of age

Cut back on your commitments if
you feel pressured

Every little bit counts

Don't whine

The more maneuverable ship should give way to the less maneuverable craft

Don't deny anyone the opportunity to do something nice for you

Experience is the true educator

When you are good to others, you are best to yourself

It's all in how you look at it

Life is broken down into a series of instances

Work hard to make a difference

Listen with an open heart

If you do nothing, nothing will happen

Life is like a wave: ride it to the shore

Nothing can truly be taken from us; there is nothing to lose

Common sense is a philosophy

If you wish for a thing and do not get it, try working for it

Time means everything

Snowflakes are some of nature's most fragile things—but look what they can do when they stick together

A library is a repository of medicine for the mind

Hope is the best defense for old age

Chase happiness

Keep your receipts

A change of scenery makes for good health

There comes an age in everyone's life when the only person you fool is yourself

Rediscover an appreciation for the big and small things in life

Welcome change

There are many branches to the tree of knowledge

Time is a resource to be used creatively

By pursuing any one of our dreams, we can find fulfillment

Appreciate the simple

Travel light

Walk forward

Gaining knowledge and wisdom is pleasurable

Keep your composure after each mischance

The process is the reality

Tell at least one person each day that you like, admire, or appreciate her

Small people do small things

Fulfill your dreams

Talk is cheap

Easy does it

When you are right, you can afford to keep your temper

Our current life is our future generation's history

Once a crook, always a crook

Allow yourself to have fun

Humor can hurt just as easily as make someone laugh

Praise does wonders for a person's sense of hearing

Make the best decisions that you can based on the best information that you can gather at the time

Hang on to your dreams

There will never be enough time, but there will be the time you need

Know how to forget

Choose your mate as you choose your shoes—for comfort and long wear

Remember to return borrowed items

No one can tell you how long you should mourn

Dream boldly

The greatest joy is in creating

Be good for something

Being able to live with yourself is more important than anything else

Become a visionary thinker

Trust yourself when it comes to questions on how to live

Those who look up see the stars

Don't try to please everybody

Whenever everybody tends to
his own business, news is scarce

Too much liquor makes strange
things happen

He enjoys life who makes others
enjoy it

Maintain inner peace in a world
of turmoil

Love remembered is never lost

Don't get complacent

Masterpieces are intended to
be shared

The test of someone's breeding is
how she behaves in a quarrel

What goes up must come down

Divide your grief by sharing it with
a friend

Laws need to be supported by the
people

Love makes both people stronger
together than if they were
separate

Don't be too open-minded

If things do not feel right, take time
to think and seek improvements

The brave man is daring enough to
forgive an injury

Sit down for a family meal at least
once a day

Do not let a day pass without
making at least one person
feel good

Trees that bend survive longer than
trees that break in the wind

Walk around ladders

Roam

See things as they are

You don't get a second chance to
make a good first impression

Don't sabotage yourself

The headline of a story may not tell
the whole story

Time dilutes anger

Poetry gives meaning to important
feelings we have but cannot
define

Live your life in a manner that
never infringes on the happiness
of others

Saying hi to a stranger can result in
a new friend

Every road has hills

Life is too short to nurse animosities
or register wrongs

Begin where you are

It is easier to be wealthy and
powerful than it is to be beautiful

Develop the ability to solve problems

Never be too proud to turn back

You're never too old to learn

The service we give others is the rent
we pay for our room on earth

It is up to you to make your life great

Don't get bogged down with chores

Always have more love than money

Mystery is about perception

Make sure you pay enough attention
to yourself

The happiest people on earth are
happy old people

A sunny disposition can brighten
a cloudy day

It is easy to make a fool of yourself

Relax for a moment, the work will
still be there

If you are easily burned, do not go
near the fire

Go to bed when you're tired

The classroom is the frontier of
freedom

Demonstration is the best mode of
instruction

The more you lean on somebody else,
the leaner are your chances for
success

The young have the same enemy as
the old: time

Grow all the time

One of the greatest lessons in life
is learning to be happy without
the things we cannot or should
not have

Be served by others as little as
    possible

This is a great time if you know
    what to do with it

What people can think up is limitless

Do what you really want to do for
    work

Write forgiveness letters right
    away—or later if you need time

The greatest achievements are those
    that benefit others

Fear and hope are great motivators

The way to conquer death is to lead
    a happy life

Better praise yourself than find fault
    with others

Be a citizen of the world

Profit from good advice

Read the classics

Talk happiness

Blessed are the flexible for they shall
    not get bent out of shape

Most people do not recognize how
  free they are

Smile, look at, and say hello to
  strangers

Reach out in love

You cannot love without giving

Children gravitate to gentle souls

Keep your feet on the ground

If you take care of your character,
  your reputation will take care
  of itself

Accidents will happen

All for one, and one for all
  (Alexandre Dumas)

Beware of danger signals

All heroes started out as ordinary
  people

Politeness costs nothing and gains
  everything

You can always make room for
  happiness

You can never get too much of
  a good thing

Don't always play it safe

Every day is a new day

See magic in the mundane

Know how to find out what you
don't know

Take pleasure in pathless woods

Time is the most expensive
commodity

Earnest effort leads to success

Fill your life with love

Surprising others is a particularly
rich joy

Achieving happiness is the beginning
of experiencing happiness

In skating over thin ice, our safety
is in our speed

Some things need to be said

Behavior is a mirror in which
everyone shows his image

Give your best to your employer

If you want a friend, you will have
to be one

Knowing your faults is a strength

To think is to live

Take the bitter with the sweet

Don't wait too long to call a doctor

Real unselfishness consists of
sharing the interests of others

A good book can change a person's
life

Nighttime seems to last longer than
daytime

He who seeks a quarrel will find it

Your image of yourself is different in
your mind than in the minds of
others

You cannot go far in a rowboat
without oars

Welcome what chance brings

Compliment yourself constantly

Most people know other people's
faults better than their own

Nothing is as powerful as the
moment a person learns
something from a mistake

One lie leads to another

Having knowledge and using knowledge are two totally different things

Do everything to bring elegance, order, beauty, and joy into each task you perform

Eloquence is the child of knowledge

Don't forget to count your blessings

Invite fears to stay briefly, then send them away

Living life is an education

It is better to pay and have a little less than to have much and be always in debt

Take it easy on yourself

Criticism usually hurts more than it helps

A place for everything and everything in its place

Patience and passage of time do more than strength and fury

Memories enable you to live something again

Patience is the best remedy for every
trouble

It is sometimes beneficial to forget
what you know

One good turn deserves another

Catch a good sunset from
time to time

Change the inner attitudes
of your mind to change
the outer aspects of your life

Playing well with other children
prepares you to work well with
others as an adult

Don't tempt fate

Life has a different meaning to each
person

People make history

Do not jest in serious matters

The true value of life cannot be
measured in dollars

History explains why we are where
we are

It is as much fun hiking through
the woods as it is staying at
a fancy resort

Do nothing in malice

A certain smell can bring you back to
your youth

If you cannot command yourself,
you cannot command others

Be moderate even in moderation

A complete person does not accuse
others of creating his misfortunes

There are no laws for love

The good you do to others will
always come back to you

Your expression is the most
important thing you can wear

Every advantage has its
disadvantage

Strong people do not need a lot of
other people around

Give snakes the right of way

Be efficient in transacting business

You can't be a hero without taking
chances

Accept things as they are, not as you
wish them to be

Be faster to make up than to fight

It takes more courage to live than
to die

Best friends begin where the
individuals leave off

Slow down

Never underestimate your enemy

The good seaman can be recognized
when the storm comes

Work and love with commitment

Be mostly silent

It is never too late to start reading

Commit to your choice, over and over

You can always become smarter

Life should not be looked back at
bitterly

If you have to do it every day, for
God's sake learn to do it well

Don't quit before the finish line

Live and let live

No matter how far you have gone
down the wrong road, turn back

The crisis of yesterday is the joke
of tomorrow

Do not disguise yourself to others

Doing the best at this moment puts
you in the best place for the next
moment

Read the fine print

Good books create good ideas

Life is a blank canvas and you are
the artist

Being human is a privilege,
not an excuse

Circumstances cannot affect true
love

Learn about love

Be patient for answers to come
to you

One thing leads to another

Neither abstinence nor excess ever
renders man happy

Most crises present opportunities

Take the time to listen

Give people a second chance

Do not complain about something if
you had the power to change it
but did not

Love occurs less than most people
will admit

Other people cannot insult you
unless you allow them to

Understand the history that gave us
our freedom

It is better to be decisive, even if
sometimes you are wrong

Face the truth

A good salesperson treats you exactly
as you want everyone to treat you

Worry more about things you can
control than about things you
cannot control

Providence helps those who
help themselves

Every fish that escapes
seems bigger than it is

Lawyers are usually the only ones
to benefit from divorce

Too few know when they possess
enough, and fewer know how
to enjoy it

Every right implies a responsibility

An interesting person can make the
mundane seem interesting

Forgiving gives a person strength

The voice of experience keeps its
mouth shut

Even if you are on the right track,
you will get run over if you just
sit there (Will Rogers)

Let your thoughts be noisy, colorful,
and lively

Take criticism and praise with equal
grace

Add new elements to your life

Good times are better when shared

Dream in color

There are no true absolute rights or
wrongs in life

Sometimes it is easy for love to turn
into hate

Cooperation is doing with a smile
what you have to do anyway

Adapt well to nature

Find out where your path begins

It is later than you think

Good management works as well in
a place of business as at home

True knowledge gives you the tools
to recognize what you know and
do not know

Never yield to the pressures of the
masses

Great empires have been brought
down by a moment's stupidity

The sense of living is joy enough

Fences mean nothing to those who
can fly

Giving love is an education in itself

Joy is the ability to be happy in
small ways

Nature is the best way to learn about
change

Don't confuse inconveniences with
　problems

Keep your face to the sunshine
　and you cannot see the
　shadows

Take two minutes to breathe deeply

Dream big

To teach is to learn twice

Laugh at your mistakes

Before blame, see if you can excuse

We may give advice but we cannot
　inspire conduct

Government is the servant of the
　people and not their master

Parents need to be strong-willed and
　broad-minded at the same time

Let there be many windows to
　your soul

You can't force someone to like you

When you put your energy behind
　something, the results will be
　powerful

Wisdom is knowing what to do next, skill is knowing how to do it, and virtue is doing it

Every second you are alive gives you the opportunity to live your life

Encourage others to talk about themselves

Enemies can be useful

There is no need to have to prove anything to anyone else

True love is better expressed with action rather than words

Minor stress does not have to be overwhelming

Coolness comes naturally to cool people

Controlling your life means controlling your time

You must understand before you can learn

Money does not buy class

Losing weight should not be a full-time job

Stop when you cannot go on anymore

If you want knowledge, you must work for it

A dream is always better than the achievement

Cope with illness

Occasionally do something unusual

Enthusiasm needs to come naturally

All people are poets at heart

Marriage is a fifty-fifty proposition

Children understand bribery at an early age

Learn from life's low moments

Anyone can make an oath, only the true can keep it

Ask yourself if what you're doing today is getting you closer to where you want to be tomorrow

By changing, a person can achieve consistency

Making friends is an art

A good childhood appears to go by quickly

Ask questions you do not know
   the answers to

Life is made up of surprises

First impressions rule the mind

Hate is created by fears

Decide to be extraordinary and do
   what you need to do

Wear your learning like your watch,
   in a private pocket

A closed mouth gathers no foot

A rising tide will lift all boats

You will know what is more than
   enough before you will know
   what is enough

Prevention is the first step of cure

Seize the first opportunity to act on
   every resolution you make

Don't give voice to any and every
   passing feeling or thought

Be insatiably curious

Never is a long time

Each man is the architect of his
   own fate

Few can walk alone

Learn even from an enemy

Grieve only when you are in pain; don't anticipate it

Don't get upset just because everyone else is

Say "please" and "thank you" liberally

Find your destiny

Feather your own nest

Moderation in everything except love

Thinking is the hardest thing in the world to do

Never try out a new recipe on guests

Life should be too short to do all the things you want to do

Hunger is the first course to a good dinner

Watching television is an excuse for not doing something

Share the spotlight whenever possible

A shallow person is easily satisfied

It is better to be a coward for a
minute than dead for the rest
of your life

The sweetest grapes hang highest

Become more aware of all that is
possible

Posture says a lot about self-
confidence

Wealth is having all the money you
need, not want

Always act well the part that is
given to you

Find truth in your life

Whoever does wrong, wrongs himself

Eating should not be about
rewarding yourself

Make life exciting

Hope is always just around
the corner

Privacy is a right

Most new fashions are
old fashions reinvented

You cannot force a free person

Do not count your fish before you catch them

The fear of death is worse than dying

Too much of life is spent waiting for moments

In a relationship, love must be constant

Let your nose go in front, but do not always follow it

The most difficult part about working out is going to the gym

Do something nice for someone who will never find out about it

Other people's expectations may not be yours

Work enjoyed is as much fun as leisure

Let bygones be bygones

Do not expect to be acknowledged for what you are

There is no accounting for taste

To care is to share

Compromise is essential in everyday life

Take care of your body

There is no one definition of success

Forget about yourself and go about your work

Be sober and temperate, and you will be healthy

Entertain great hopes

We do well not to grieve often

Exercise your soul

Experience more happiness than drama in life

Use technology to simplify your life, not make it more complicated

Rejuvenate yourself by being alone

Even if you are afraid, do it anyway

He who wishes to be forgiven must forgive

Knowledge is the treasure of the mind

Be the person you thought you would be when you were young

If you worry about having enough, you never will have enough

You give but little when you give of
  your possessions

Ask a lot out of life

Do not turn up your trousers before
  you get to the brook

Kisses are the language of love

Think of your problems as potential
  teachers

Consider the source

You cannot change human nature

Always listen to the other side

It depends on what you are made of
  whether you take on a polish or
  get worn down

The institute of the family seems to
  work out very well

Beware of borrowing

Doing the right thing will gratify
  some people and astonish the rest

Strive to become better

Complain to the right people

Old age should be grown into

By living life, a wise person becomes wiser

Having a good reputation is invaluable

The first half of your life you try to kill yourself, the second half you try to stay alive as long as possible

Everything is the result of change

The harder the battle, the sweeter the victory

Give others opportunities to be generous

Give birth to your own potential

Children are not little adults

The key to communications is saying something in a way that your audience can understand it

Make peace with imperfection

The best way to not die is to live

Live by your standards, not other people's standards

Test ideas first to make sure they work

Absence is like the wind for lovers apart—it can either blow out a fire or fan the flame

No work is ever wasted if it expresses something important to you

Clean out a different drawer or closet every week

You cannot lay remorse upon the innocent nor lift it from the heart of the guilty

Read, hear, or see great works during each day

Most people are not the same at the beginning of a marriage as they are during it

Tears are agents of healing

Never worry alone

You and your work will suffer if you are not happy with your job

He is lucky who forgets what cannot be mended

Nature does nothing uselessly

Each person values life differently

Do not waste time responding to your critics

When you pursue something, do so with grace, finesse, and flexibility

A good bargain is no bargain if you do not need the thing

The view is unique at the top of the mountain

Man depends on nature as much as nature depends on man

Avoid adopting other people's negative views

Try to succeed by merit

Improve yourself today

The happy highway, though never straight, is often scenic

Reading is like flying . . . in your mind

Think noble thoughts

He who buys what he does not need steals from himself

Junk is anything that has outlived its usefulness

If you are wrong, admit it quickly and emphatically

Better to fall down on the job than to lie down

It requires more courage not to fight than to fight

If you can determine where to begin, then you have solved 90 percent of the problem

Success may come with strings attached

Hindsight is 20-20

It is hard to work for money you spend on things you don't really need

Don't let fashion rule you

Birds of a feather flock together

Along with age comes freedom

If we don't change, we don't grow

A true friend is with you in the bad times as well as the good ones

In arguments, fight fair

It is the empty space within the
vessel that makes it useful
(Tao Te Ching)

Reading maketh a full man

Pay attention to your thoughts,
behaviors, and values and work
on what you need to change

Plunge boldly into the thick of life

Let nothing limit you

The best dreams occur when we are
awake

Cherish your old friends

It is better to do than to talk about
doing

Go on a retreat once a year

Wisdom influences attitudes and
opinions

Teach yourself to have fewer wants

All events contain an advantage for
you, if you look for it

Forgiveness is the ultimate lesson

Dying makes room for the young

It is amazing how long it takes to complete something you are not working on

Ask for a third opinion

Remember that life is not an emergency

There are three kinds of people: the wills, the won'ts, the can'ts

Do more than you thought possible

Friendships need constant care

Death puts life into perspective

Life is funny

Gardens are down-to-earth

Read the best books first

Value yourself above others

If you want to gather honey, don't kick over the beehive

A wise person admits she has faults

Have the spirit of conquest

As the master is, so is his dog

Strike a good balance between work and play

Adults usually forget how children think and feel

Share your imagination

It is better to have a little than to have nothing

Live life with compassion and understanding

Well-adjusted parents raise well-adjusted children

Do not push your victories too far

Read documents carefully that require a signature

Tasting life is life's gift

It is easier to recognize when you are sick than when you are healthy

When you are happy, do not look too far ahead

Absence sharpens love, presence strengthens it

To be successful in love, one must know how to begin and when to stop

Remember your promises

Real healing occurs in the soul

Love your children unconditionally

Accept that everything worthwhile
    is challenging

Time is nature's way of keeping
    everything from happening
    at once

Donate blood

Life should not be lived with eyes
    half shut

Dare to be naïve

Too much flattering is just as bad as
    not enough

In avoiding one evil, care must be
    taken to not fall into another

Money does not guarantee anything

You cannot know what is best for
    anyone but yourself

Take note of your own faults
    and leave others' alone

Poetry is to be enjoyed like
    a good glass of wine

Smiling is cheaper than plastic
    surgery

The chief function of the body is to carry the brain around

If you are too busy to laugh, you are too busy

Friendship is love with understanding

Home is the resort of love, joy, and plenty

Determine your priorities according to the situation you are in

Find ways to forget things that are cluttering your mind

Respect your environment

Do not feel guilty when you outgrow a love or a friendship

Make sure your feelings are true

Anxiety breeds anxiety

Answer the easy questions first

Take good care of those you love

Strengths become stronger when used properly

Don't squander your energy

Teach your kids to eat right and
be healthy

No one can tell you how to think

Protect your enthusiasm from the
negativity of others

Feeling good about yourself is a sign
of success

The happiest people seem to be those
who have no particular reason
for being happy except that they
are so

Love is the foundation for life

Save money when you need to least

Hurry makes life go by faster

Search for new perspectives

Candor breeds hatred

A lie runs until it is overtaken by
the truth

Even small children have a right
to privacy

Enthusiasm is as contagious as
the common cold

Imagination is more important than
knowledge (Albert Einstein)

Make a will

Society fails when there is a great distance between the very rich and the very poor

The best cure for drunkenness is to see a drunken person while sober

Love knows no boundaries

After a big adventure everything tastes and smells better

Live the life you have imagined

Delay ill health as long as possible

Ask questions that other people will enjoy answering

Some people have it in them to triumph while others do not

Spend your energy creating the life you desire

Character matters more than reputation

The love of flattery and pride is a disease of the mind

Practice what you preach

Pass on more than our genes to our children

Love consists not in gazing at each other but in looking outward in the same direction

Commit yourself to quality

Rather a slip of the foot than a slip of the tongue

The true joy in life is being used for a purpose recognized by yourself as a mighty one

You cannot get a quart into a pint jar

Worry about the right things, not the wrong things

Prefer depth to breadth

Goodness is the only investment that never fails

What is difficult and challenging enhances our growth

Write your own epitaph, then live to make it true

Create space for others in your life

If you don't want things to change, then don't change what you are doing

The man who does not demand his
rights is buried alive

Money needs wisdom in order to
be kept

With each day, try to do what seems
best for that day

Hear the other side

Losing an illusion makes you wiser
than finding a truth

Try to stay ahead of events

Realize when a mistake has been
made

See the difference between success
and the appearance of success

No one else will do it for you

It is a good thing when youth is
restless

Days are miles in the voyage of life

Improve your wardrobe by getting
in shape

Bear an injury in silence rather than
provoke a thousand by flying into
a rage

Remember to smile when you
wake up

You are the captain of your soul

Bring flowers inside

If little ears should not hear it, then
big mouths should not say it

Be sure; a lie will find you out

Make two lists: things you have to do
and things you want to do

Letting children grow and raising
them are two different things

Impatience gathers unripe fruit

Inspiration creates energy

Create a worthwhile purpose in life

The desire to live makes life last
longer

Never agree to surrender your
dreams

Cook with tender loving care

Make your actions match your
good intentions

Moderation in all things

Cut sugar consumption

Life is like a bicycle: you do not fall off unless you stop peddling

Be a friend to yourself first

Live content with small means

A fool does not learn from his own mistakes

Overload results in chaos and even sickness

Bring the beginning, middle, and end into agreement

It is never too late to start over

Eat moderately

Stupidity has no limits

Life delights in life

Be willing to resist anything that takes you off your chosen path

No one has a patent on happiness

Work makes life sweet

No one is in complete control of what happens in his life

Being happy or being miserable is what separates most people

Life is all about dealing with
  unknowns

Aggressive talk lowers you in the
  esteem of your acquaintances

Looking up is a better habit than
  looking down

The past can chain you up, but the
  future can set you free

Boys will be boys

Enlarge your world by finding more
  affinities and potencies in objects
  you already have

If you cannot catch a fish, do not
  blame the sea

Friends are lost by calling too often
  and calling too seldom

Take what you can use and let the
  rest go by

Try to view the place you live in like
  a tourist does on vacation

The first blow does not fell the tree

Brighten the space wherever you are

Laugh out loud

Improve your performance by
improving your attitude

Nurture friendships

Keep working as long as you can

Sometimes the only way to make
amends is to change the
way we live

Get up early three mornings
and you'll gain a half day

Don't give up on anybody

If at first you do not succeed, you are
about average

Having a habit does not necessarily
mean it is right

Pursue worthy aims

Your children are with you, yet they
do not belong to you

Pass on to others what you have
learned in life

A good education opens many doors

Be there when people need you

Excuses keep you away from
achieving your goals

Life is not a cup to be drained,
but a measure to be filled

Attach yourself to what is spiritually
superior

Jump into the unknown to avoid
complacency

Absolute power corrupts absolutely

The course of true love never did run
smooth (Shakespeare)

By falling, we learn to go safely

Do more today to see what your
limits really are

Tap into your creativity

Love makes hard hearts gentle

Knowledge is received; wisdom is
gained

When you most feel like moping,
do something—anything

Do not wake misfortune while
she sleeps

The problem is not to learn, but to
unlearn

Eat slowly

He that climbs the tall tree has
a right to the fruit

Dispose of the barriers to your
dreams

Never be afraid to dare

A good reputation is more valuable
than money

It is a poor frog who does not play in
his own pond

Our friends are our mirrors and
show us ourselves

When we do the best we can, we
never know what miracles await

The bait hides the hook

Silence is a true friend who never
betrays

Appreciate all the help you can get
along the way

Families cannot be picked

There are always two sides to every
story

Feelings are useless without words

Stack two layers of praise around
every critique

It is all right to love someone more
than he loves you

When one must, one can

Everybody should believe in
something

You carry the key to release
you from your own chains

Imagine success

Do not cry till you are hurt

Learn to survive defeat

Nothing brings you peace but
yourself

Absence may make the heart grow
fonder, but presence makes the
heart stronger

Easy to anger, easy to forgive

You cannot pay somebody to practice
for you

There are plenty of other fish in
the sea

To see the small is to have insight

Accept temporary inconvenience for
a permanent improvement

Every man is the guardian of his own honor

Great books are lived not read

Pay attention to the people you love

Think of something original

Most things get better by themselves

The soul lives longer than the body

Spend money when you have it most

Forget blunders and absurdities as soon as you can

We must have infinite faith in each other

A genius is a crackpot whose crazy idea actually works

Beginnings are brand-new chances

In order to receive, you must give

Get involved with your local government

Think through things to the conclusion

Sometimes your opinion needs to be altered

Don't sacrifice or deny your convictions

Show malice toward no one

Do not count too much on friends

A good snapshot stops a moment from running away

In the end, all will mend

The grateful man gets more than he asks

Nobody can take your dreams away

The future is uncertain; the past is certain

The house praises the carpenter

You cannot tell how deep a puddle is until you step in it

Belong to yourself

Nothing is impossible to a willing mind

Do not think small

Weed your own garden first

The smallest deed is better than the grandest intention

There is nothing so kingly as
   kindness and nothing so royal
   as truth

Three strikes and you're out

Nothing comes out that is not put in

Criticism should rectify errors or
   improve judgment

Knowledge is the basis of life

The remedy for bad times is to be
   patient with them

We cannot feel what is in another
   person's heart

Everyone has unhappy experiences
   throughout life

Always carry identification

Kids will be kids

Happy the man who can call today
   his own

Every person is the architect of his
   own fortune

Use no hurtful deceit

Flowers are nature's poetry

Always look out for number one
and be careful not to step on
number two

Liars never prosper

A good education requires more than
just going to school

The worst thing to do to a child is to
embarrass him

Intelligence needs experience in
order to thrive

Be truthful, merciful, and intelligent

You can drown in your own dreams

Be all that you can be

Do not let your superiors know you
are better than them

An excuse can sometimes be more
damaging than saying nothing
at all

Genius is its own end

Being around certain people can
make you miserable

There is a time for all things

When you listen to people, know how to distinguish between the smart ones and the fools

Success and failure come from within

It is never too late in life to make a new start

The mind transforms an experience into a lesson

When both people work at a marriage, it becomes twice as good

What is beautiful to one person may be ugly to another

Nothing on this earth lasts forever

The stream returns to its source

Diligence brings delight

Value all life

Keep looking ahead

The only good thing about anger is it proves you have feelings

We are always learning, always growing

All debt is wiped out upon death

Be aware of the snowball effect of
your thinking

You are in love when you do not have
to ask anyone else if you are

Do good deeds to benefit another
generation

The only certainty is that nothing is
certain (Pliny the Elder)

A fool can be popular

Genius is 1 percent inspiration
and 99 percent perspiration
(Thomas Alva Edison)

The best antique is an old friend

Life is like an onion: you peel off one
layer at a time and sometimes
you cry

The situation may not always be
what it appears

It is easier to be happy when you are
healthy than when you are sick

Notice your chances in life

Don't let someone else tell you your
dreams cannot be achieved

Every generation has its foolish
  moments

Learn a lesson every time you lose

Respect other people's privacy

Hoping is free

Improve with age

No pleasure lasts if it's unseasoned
  by variety

Your internal age can be very
  different from your external age

Even a guilty conscience can be
  justified

The more you listen to the voice
  within you, the better you will
  hear what is sounding outside
  (Dag Hammarskjöld)

Power does not like to lose

See no evil, hear no evil,
  speak no evil

It is hard to fight an enemy who has
  outposts in your head

Television is not reality

Have faith in yourself

Nothing can bring you peace but
    yourself

Imagine that everyone is enlightened

The only way to determine if a
    person has courage is to test her

Behind seeming permanence lies
    constant flux

It is better to be wounded than
    to walk in armor

Believe in love

Two simple words, *yes* and *no,*
    require the most thought
    before use

Love is the world that frees us of all
    the weight and pain of life

Once the mind is sound, it is easier
    to make the body fit

Since we expect more from friends,
    it takes us longer to forgive them

You know you understand things
    when you can give without being
    asked

Everyone can use a prayer

It is the bait that lures, not the
    fisherman or the reel

Eat inspiring foods

Believe in love at first sight

When you arrive, you will know you
    are there

When you get older, you realize your
    parents did the best job that they
    could under the circumstances

Do not fly off the handle

Have patience with yourself

Major decisions should not be made
    when you feel too tired

Do not be afraid of tomorrow; look at
    what could happen today

Enjoy the physical aspects of
    your day

Negotiate with others as you would
    like them to negotiate with you

He who sees his own faults is too
    busy to see the faults of others

Time does heal

Freedom is its own reward

The more creative you are, the more fun your children will have

Reach out for support

There is no one correct formula for living a good life

Celebrations should be an expression of joy

Love is a great catalyst for creativity

It is not the house that makes the home, it is the love that is inside

Every good deed you do genuinely comes back to you in abundance

Making a living is not the same as making a life

If you carry yourself like a beauty, people will think of you as one

If it's not working, stop doing it

It is truly never too late

When you're through learning, you're through

Dare to live

When arguing, never resort to personal abuse

Not everything is all peaches and
   cream

No two people read the same book

Connect with life

Patience is one of the best skills
   to have

Make yourself worth knowing

Beauty is only gene deep

Find yourself in the present moment

Perhaps you hear a different
   drummer, so step to the music
   you hear

Learn about yourself from your
   children

Life is about learning

After dinner take a walk

Have but a few confidants

There are more worthless people
   alive than worthy ones

There is more than one correct way
   to raise children

A good name is better than fine
   jewels

Open your eyes

You can never get all the possums up
the same tree

More are drowned in drink than
in water

A strong body makes the mind strong

Inspired people get more
accomplished

Look for simple solutions first

Have a tender heart

You need to love in order to be loved

When embarrassed, stop talking and
thinking about it and move on to
something else

It is important to develop character
along with your mind

Fulfill the dreams of your youth

Some people just know more

No one else has the answers to your
unique set of problems

The higher you go, the better
the view

A book is like a garden carried in
   the pocket

Enjoy companionship

You are unique

Be a good winner

The opportunity of a lifetime is
   seldom so labeled

Anything can happen

If you love your work, you will do
   a good job

Don't postpone life

Strength simplifies things that seem
   impossible

Do the business at hand first

Allow your mind to solve problems
   while you are busy doing
   something else

Memories make a lot of mistakes

Everyone cannot be first

Almost every wise saying has an
   opposite one

Love begins from within

Occasionally, a lie that spares
a person pain is better than
a truth that hurts

The best remedy for a short temper
is a long walk

Where there's smoke, there's fire

Be silent or say something better
than silence

Work worth doing is not work

Freedom is taken for granted until it
is taken away

The world stands still for lovers

If you look hard enough, you can find
good in everything

Deal with people honestly

Misfortune makes us wise

A dog does not resent being called
a dog

You cannot fit a round peg in
a square hole

Make others feel important

When sad, think of something funny

The simplest task is meaningful if
done in the right spirit

Quiet people get the benefit of
the doubt

A person is what he is under
pressure

A curiosity is the first step to a great
accomplishment

The heart has a major influence on
the brain

Someone will always be looking
at you as an example of how
to behave

You can always learn something from
a child

A good conversationalist lets the
other person do most of the
talking

Do not remain on the outside
looking in

A nap can cure a lot of things

It's hard to argue with someone
when she's right

Long is not forever

Marriage is not the difficult part, it
is the living together that is hard

Praise is always welcome

People who enjoy life tend to live
longer

Start over every morning

Life becomes less complex when you
eliminate needless wants

Comedy is medicine

Ask yourself, what's really
important?

Where the needle goes, the thread
follows

Books can change the way we think

Playtime is essential

Live without regrets

There are many echoes in the world,
but few voices (Goethe)

Answer the phone with enthusiasm

Having superior information gives
you an advantage over your peers

Experience the present moment

Anyone who reaches out for help is
entitled to your compassion and
attention

It is cheaper to be your own
psychiatrist

A person's reputation can be ruined
by one lie

If you retire, find something else to
do—something you can pursue
as if it were a livelihood

Bad days eventually end

Curiosity is the mark of a vigorous
intellect

Almost everything can be interpreted
in a different way

When people know that you believe
in them, wondrous things begin
to happen

Wide experience makes for deep
tolerance

Have patience with a friend rather
than lose him forever

Keep your troubles to yourself

Like a fence, character cannot be
    strengthened by whitewash

When the game is over, let it be over

One person's danger is another
    person's fun

Contradict with respect

Silence teaches you the joys of sound

What we least expected generally
    happens

If you do not fear death, then you do
    not fear anything

Books allow us to time travel

Honesty is the first chapter of
    the book of wisdom

Ignore negative thoughts

It is better to bind your children to
    you by a feeling of respect and
    gentleness than by fear

Curiosity can solve many problems

Know when to speak up

Don't use name-calling in fights

Many small good moments outweigh
    one big good event

Many great inventions and ideas
have come during leisure time

Observe and feel as many different
things as you can

Conquering fear is the beginning of
wisdom

Stretch your mind

Read books about subjects unknown
to you

Ask questions

Don't buy groceries when you are
hungry

Say what you really mean

Make sure you have all the facts
before you begin to worry

Choose your battles wisely

Give people the benefit of the doubt

Most of us know how to say nothing;
few of us know when

Feed your body less and your mind
more

Lightning can strike twice

Have pleasure in giving pleasure

Success is the end of a process

Our greatest deeds we do
   unknowingly

Everything we see has the potential
   to teach us something

Always leave them laughing

If you throw a handful of stones,
   at least one will hit

In order for love to work, it needs to
   be returned

The only thing we truly possess in
   life is time

The worst excuse is "I did it because
   everyone else did"

When you speak, do it in a manner
   that dignifies you

Resign yourself to the influences of
   each season

Feel young when you are young

A person's worth is no greater than
   the worth of her ambitions

Life is full of mysteries

To be content, look to those who possess less, not those who possess more

Profit from doing what you love

Forgive yourself and others

Don't respond to your critics

It is stressful and a lot of work to hold a grudge

It takes two flints to make a fire

Look inside yourself for the strength to continue

A happy young person will be a happy old person

Spend more time doing than preparing

In this world nothing is certain but death and taxes (Benjamin Franklin)

Pleasure is very seldom found where it is sought

Gather pretty things for your house

Little boats should stay close to shore

It is easier to feel failure than it is to feel success

Make happiness a habit

Don't think about death too much

Be industrious and frugal and you will be rich

Some people require praise more than others

Rest is not important to the busy

A man is known by the company he keeps

Adventures can change your life

Tell a lie once to someone and you are always a liar to that person

Try to fix any problem you have caused

Heal yourself

Forgive your enemies

Embrace the past with remembrance and the future with longing

Build a margin of safety

Some of the most creative ideas come from beginners

A book is the cheapest way to travel

Be careful who you laugh at

Everyone has something she
  yearns for

Lose yourself in your work

It is no use crying over spilt milk

Do things with your children while
  they still want to do things with
  you

Power can corrupt

Don't let a rut become a grave

Nothing is politically right that is
  morally wrong

Nothing gets you nothing

Don't take what you cannot use

An actor is only as good as his
  audience

Good art is best when shared

Childhood should be happy and
  carefree

Let your fears fly free

Never neglect older people

Don't venture out of your depth till
you can swim

Reinterpret the past

Wake up and appreciate everything
you encounter along your path

If the conversation around you is
decaying, lead it to more
constructive subjects

A minute of extra thinking
beforehand can save hours
of worry later

Make sure your family feels
connected

It is easier to say "no" first and
change it to "yes" than it is to say
"yes" first and change it to "no"

As time progresses, we become
different people

Life is a mirror

After sorrow comes joy

Endure uncertainty

Be good and happy today

Know when not to do anything

Let your child find her own
uniqueness within herself

Turn a hobby into a job

A garden, like a child, needs more
than just planting in order to
grow

The past can only come back through
memories

Life is either a daring adventure or
nothing (Helen Keller)

Absurdity appears to be more the
rule than the exception

It is better to be nobly remembered
than nobly born

Many small problems equal one big
problem

Good parents make mistakes, too

Many inventions are accidents

Know where you are going

Take responsibility for your actions

As you make your bed, so you must
lie in it

Every age brings new opportunities

Hold your head high

Keep up appearances

Gaining experience means making mistakes

Challenge yourself on your own ideas, and if they still appear to be good ideas, then they probably are

Do not forget to dream

It is better to be a failure at something you love than to be a success at something you hate

Many things can be said without using words

All things are difficult before they are easy

Life's big chances rarely give advance warning

Don't allow self-pity

Time is supposed to go by

You cannot make others as you wish them to be

Modest speech makes your message stronger

You may delay, but time will not

Each person deserves the land he takes up

You can fill a house with the things you bought but do not use or need

Be happy while you are alive

Economy is the prime requisite of a sound financial plan

Raise patience to a passion

You can't have everything you want or think you want

Gravitate toward a more balanced lifestyle

Make sure you can distinguish between the show and the advertisements

Establish a simple bedtime routine for kids

Most lies have an essence of the truth

The more possessions, the more worry

Strive for self-mastery

Understand what guides you

Whether the road goes uphill or downhill depends on where you stand

We are a part of nature equally as much as nature is a part of us

Let your best be for your friend

Idleness is never enjoyable unless there is plenty to do

Nobody is perfect

Try to stop one heart from breaking

There is a story behind every photograph

As long as you live you must learn how to live

Great fishes are caught in great waters

You are rich according to what you are, not what you have

Things accumulate to fill space

When friends offer to help, let them

Do not holler before you are hurt

Do not wait until you are lost to begin to find yourself

Sharing your life with your children as friends is the greatest and most enjoyable experience you can have

Nothing is certain

Doing two things at the same time takes twice as long

Great minds discuss ideas, average minds discuss events, small minds discuss people

Nothing stays the same

Be sure you know the road before you act as guide

Intelligence requires freedom

Intimacy breeds contempt

Freedom is in the mind

Hope, but not too extravagantly

Sometimes you need an ending in order to start a new beginning

Sometimes people prefer a lie to the truth

Have perseverance and confidence in
 yourself

The world must be taken as it is

Nothing is beautiful from every point
 of view

Just because two people argue, it
 does not mean they do not love
 each other

Idealism precedes experience

Even the most menial task done, if
 done with passion, is rewarding

The greatest physician is optimism

Greatness can appear in tiny and
 large ways

Showing anger is a sign of weakness

Live more fully while you can

We make more enemies by what we
 say than friends by what we do

Success is not permanent and failure
 is not fatal

You can be as free as your mind
 lets you

Be the person of your dreams

Knots are more easily tied than
untied

Have little and you will gain, have
much and you will be confused

Flow with nature, not against her

Recovery comes in steps

Keep your mouth shut and your
eyes open

Do not say no from pride or yes from
weakness

Silence preserves integrity

A life is judged by how much good a
person has brought to the world

Forcing an issue can sometimes spoil
its outcome

It takes two to start an argument

If you convince yourself that you
have found it, then you will
have truly found it

Find challenges that test you

Argue in a way that ensures your
opponent does not become an
enemy

Love temperately

Never worry about having enough

It is one thing to get educated and
    another thing to keep educated

The most powerful force on earth
    is love

The by-product of living is wisdom

Walk forward toward the future

Being around fools can make you
    look really good

Free yourself from the things you
    don't want

Everything tastes good when you are
    hungry

When you are young, you try to look
    older than your age; when you
    are old, you try to look younger
    than your age

Happiness is equilibrium

Enjoy each stage of your life

When the heart decides
    something, reason is
    not in the equation

Look for the old so as to learn
    the new

Demonstrate the truth of your basic principles

Children are the most vulnerable population of society

Lift people up

Long-lasting confidence in oneself needs to grow slowly over the years

Stay humble

Everybody is defective in some way

Let go of the idea that gentle, relaxed people can't be superachievers

All that is known is significantly less than all there is still to learn

Enjoy other people enjoying life

True love never stops growing

Don't burn your candle at both ends

The good that people do lives after them

It is difficult to define love, but easy to recognize it

The more creative you are, the more things you notice

Drive a simple car

Do your part to contribute to others' spiritual progress

Do not delay; golden moments fly

A debt is cheaper if paid quickly

Get enough sleep

Friendship is about sharing

Whoever gossips to you will gossip about you

Deal with another as you'd have another deal with you

Never cut what can be untied

True philosophy deals with facts

Slow down when life seems to be going too fast

The saddest part of growing old is losing your friends

Be the labor great or small, do it well or not at all

Do not kill the goose that laid the golden egg

Humor is an affirmation of dignity

Form your own opinions

He who has hope has everything

Before buying anything, ask if you can do without it

The test of commitment is action

Forget yesterday

Those who cannot, criticize

A successful boss takes the blame when things go bad and shares the credit when things go well

Food tastes better when you are relaxed

Death sees everyone as an equal

Much happiness is overlooked because it does not cost anything

No act of kindness is ever wasted

There is always more good to be done

The truth can be very unpopular

The second time around should be done with fewer mistakes

You cannot change the past, but you can change the future

If you hesitate, you can still go forward

Chide not severely nor punish
hastily

We master fortune by accepting it

Manicure the wilderness

Speak only with good purpose and
think before you speak

The greatest gift to give is a gift of
your time

A question can have more meaning
than an answer

Memories can transport you back
in time

Think and speak well of others

Extreme good looks can be a curse

When you go to bed with a clear
head, you will never rise with
a headache

One always has time enough, if only
one applies it well (Goethe)

Help make your life better

Always be aware of the consequences

War represents failure

By knowing yourself, you are able to
know others

Something is lost whenever
something is gained

When you are feeling happy, enjoy it

If you kick a stone in anger, you'll
hurt your foot

We believe the things we want to
believe

Life's rewards are earned

Life should not be taken too
seriously

The eye is the painter and
the ear the singer
(Ralph Waldo Emerson)

Half a loaf is better than none

If you look for the bad in life,
you will find it

Tomorrow is not meant to be known
today

Constant complaints never get pity

Good guests know when to leave

Everyone pays for a few who make
stupid mistakes

Each life is relevant

There is not shortcut to fame

A good cry can be enjoyable

We are here to add what we can
to life, not to get what we can
from it

The wallet with lots of pictures in it
is more valuable than the one
with lots of money in it

Disorder's advantage is that, within
it, one is constantly making
discoveries

Many necessities are not necessary

There are just as many rich people
miserable as there are poor
people miserable

No one smiles in a traffic jam

Do not waste time looking at the
hill—climb it

Even the richest and most powerful
people eventually die

Like your life

Heroes are made, not born

You have to live life to love life and
you have to love life to live life

Going on adventures gives us stories
to tell that add meaning to life

Fashion is for the young; they look
better in it

Unless you show respect toward
your fellow men, you cannot
be a successful leader of men

Don't proselytize

The man who has done his best has
done everything

Inaction saps the vigors of the mind

Accentuate the positive

Bugs are bugs whether they
bite or not

Take a chance!

Forgiveness enables people to live
together

A society is only as good as its people

By remembering that life is short
you can achieve true happiness

Not all who have intelligence use it

Good health is true wealth

You can do a lot in one day

Prayers should not just be complaints

He who dances must pay the fiddler

Friendship has no rules

Find out all about yourself—there are few more important courses of study

A man who had made a mistake and doesn't correct it is making another mistake

Too much love is never enough

It pays to pester

To dispense truth is to defend freedom

Leave everything a little better than you found it

Perfection does not guarantee satisfaction

Be interested and you will be interesting

Achieving desires and wishes does not guarantee happiness

Acquire a strong will to live

Be a good loser

Great minds ask great questions

Find talents you never knew existed in you

Respect your children

Love deeply

If you want to feel good, help others

Let love come naturally

Put your fears into perspective

Common sense alone can bring you further than any other trait

Live life on purpose

Enthusiasm is caught not taught

Treat your job as important and it will be

Carry on silent conversations with yourself

Many men die at twenty-five and are not buried until they are seventy-five (Benjamin Franklin)

Live freely and die content

There are two types of people in the world: spectators and participants

We will do a lot for love

If you want something badly enough, you can get it

Be overly prepared

Do not spend your life reaching for the moon

Believe in what you are doing

People want praise more than criticism

Learn to disagree without being disagreeable

Give your energy to the one who needs it the most at that time

Let art fill you with emotions

Go the extra mile

Be angry for the right thing at the right moment and with the right amount of energy

Live your life for others as well as for yourself

Honesty in little things is a big thing

Say unexpected nice things to people

What you may do and what you ought to do are sometimes two entirely different things

Laugh at funny things

A simple lifestyle is not expensive

Go through each day without hassling anybody, without criticizing anybody, without trying to put anybody down

Jokes can make more enemies than gossip

Great people live dangerously

Avoid making sarcastic remarks

Never let the dreams die

Use the right words

In an orderly house all things are always ready

Injure others, you injure yourself

The more you give, the more you possess

Look before you or you will find yourself behind

Read to your children

Every generation stands on the shoulders of the generation that came before

Live within the rules set by nature

Possessing all that you want does not mean you have to have everything

More memories are forgotten than remembered

Action creates fate

Enjoy the little things in life naturally

A diverse population gives you the opportunity to learn many new things

Lies have a tendency to grow bigger than their original intention

Fret today, regret tomorrow

Love usually takes care of all the details

Give more in life than you take

What is true for one person may be false to another

Applying a philosophy is more important than being able to explain it

Practice the art of patience

Omit needless words

You win some, you lose some

Speak gently

Make getting older interesting

Ask for favors without being too pushy

Treat everyone as a peer

Indecision is fatal, so make up your mind

The best way to know a man is to watch him when he is angry

Ninety percent of the friction in daily life is caused by the wrong tone of voice

Forgiveness is giving love when there is no reason to

Do not add insult to injury

Adversity is a test for a strong soul

Your very best is good enough

Love makes writers write and painters paint and musicians make music

Be the kind of person that other people would want to have on their side during a war

Enjoy things because they are impermanent

Apologize immediately when you lose your temper

The game is not over until the last man strikes out

There is always room at the top

A soul cannot be measured

Television is not a substitute for life

The same person cannot be well skilled in everything; each has her special talent

Nature cures almost everything in its own time

A promise is only as valid as the person who is making it

If you can tell a little lie, then you can tell a big one, too

Stop disappointing yourself

You usually remember the simple
pleasures of life more than the
expensive pleasures

Offer a firm handshake

Jump for joy

Detours must be taken sometimes
to avoid bigger obstacles

Love can hurt as well as heal

A little knowledge on a subject can
be more dangerous than no
knowledge on the subject

Do not be down on something before
you are up on it

Learn how to be patient

There is a right way to do good

The greatest danger is to not take
the risk

Every child born possesses the
ability to change the world

The only way to defeat nature is to
live within its laws

How people treat you is more
a reflection of how they see
themselves

Youth is synonymous with hope

Home is where the heart is

Learn how to learn

It is easier to get mad than it is
to remain calm

Example is the strongest part of
education

Attention, not imitation, may be
the sincerest form of flattery

Unwritten rules are just as
important as the written ones

Beauty is in the eye of the beholder

Expect justice and goodness and
order and they will eventually
arrive

Be sympathetic to other people's
ideas and desires

Some people get paid for giving
advice while others feel they
should give it away for free

Meet adversity with hope

Speak words that are true, kind,
and constructive

Do not bore people with your
problems

Seek refinement

What is known as fact now will be
completely different in five
hundred years

Solitude cannot produce friendship

Before you buy something, think
what else you can do with that
money

Push it to the limit

Strive for accuracy

When fortune smiles, embrace her

People believe what they want to

Few people can cuss and think at the
same time

Most learning occurs from making
mistakes

Any fool can make a rule

Talk about your own mistakes
before criticizing those of
the other person

There is a lot to do before you rest

Let others be "right" most of the time

A life is not judged until it is all over

Treat the commonplace with the reverence of the sublime

A soft answer turns away wrath

Encourage your children to surpass you

Being alone is great medicine

All teenagers are cured by time

Be in a continuous state of thanksgiving

Great teams have great chemistry

Pursuing one's interests can be a full-time job

You can always catch up on work

Virtue lives forever

Remember the day you met a loved one

Choose your words carefully

If love interferes with your business, quit your business

Searching for the right answers is
the sweat work

Flee the pleasure that will pain you
tomorrow

Risk makes the reward better

Much of your pain is self-inflicted

Time has a way of contradicting
what you say

Take one's life into one's arms

He who follows another is always
behind

Everyone thinks that her children's
generation is different from hers

If you keep your clothes long enough,
they become fashionable again

Make yourself a sheep and the wolf
attacks

Exercise vigorously

Knowledge is power

Happiness is subjective

If you do not say it, you will not have
to unsay it

Put all of your eggs in one basket
and *watch that basket*

If you can't beat 'em, join 'em

Let go of beliefs that are not true

Ability, not luck, conquers

Crime does not pay

A person should spend more time
educating himself than he does
fixing himself up

Hope dies only when you die

Be thankful for success

Make money before spending it

An excessive love for anything will
cost you dearly in the end

The pure and simple truth is rarely
pure and never simple

Remember the distinction between
contribution and commitment

Clean as you go

Envision love

Know when it is time to leave
the party

Things turn out the best for people who make the best of the way things turn out

Always look people in the eye when you talk to them

Nothing important was ever achieved without someone's taking a chance

The important thing is not how much you know, but how well you know it

Don't get attached to things

Brave actions never want a trumpet

Look at all beings with compassion

When you get angry, make sure it is for the right reasons

Life is a long lesson in humility

Age is a frame of mind

Ask philosophical questions

Do not ever become something unless you want to

Do things that make you smarter

Speech is silver, silence is golden

Apathy gets you nowhere

Never do anything by halves

It is inevitable that you will age,
but it does not mean you have
to act old

Don't praise a pet unless he earns it

Talking is easy; taking action is
difficult

The tail cannot wag the dog

If it's working, keep doing it

Energy increases with happiness

Don't leave a loved one in anger

Follow your heart

Appreciate all the good times

The simplest things can inspire
greatness

Require more from yourself than
from others

Get to know what you do not know

Seeing life as an optimist is worth
much more than money

Be consistent

Those who deserve love the least are often the ones who need it the most

Speak more good things about someone behind her back than bad things

Dwelling on past pains and disappointments assures no future growth

In love, silence must be as comfortable as conversation

If you want to learn about the future, watch a child play

Never say, "You're wrong"

One bad apple will spoil the whole barrel

Respect others

Find the pleasure in working

Take everything with good humor and a grain of salt

Logic is a formal weapon

No matter how difficult our progress, we must persevere

Faith begins where reason stops

Ten men, ten minds

Brevity is the soul of wit
(Shakespeare)

Let reason hold the reins of passion

Answer questions so as not to insult
the asker

Do not spread yourself too thin

Everybody wants a little cheap
attention once in a while

Life is what you create

A happy journey almost always
depends on choosing the right
companion

Emotional needs can never be
satisfied by material items

Nothing great is created instantly

Understand yourself better than you
understand others

You do not need a higher education
to have dreams

Face your fears and name them

Perform community service with
a pure heart

Narrow your focus

Fact weighs more than opinion

You can win more friends with your ears than with your mouth

Waste nothing

Nothing is worth more than this day

Never give up

What a person says reflects her character

If you smile at people, they will almost always smile back

Life continuously swings up and down

Enjoy life

You still have a lot to learn

The chase is better than the kill

Don't expect other people to solve your problems

Be your own personal trainer

Expect nothing from he who promises a great deal

Faith is a knowledge within the heart

Your hands reveal your age

Never suppress a generous impulse

A home is strong when the
foundation is made out of love

A whole is greater than the sum of
its parts

Experience is not what happens to
you, but what you do with what
happens to you

Joy shared is doubled

Listen to yourself when you are
alone

Every living thing has something to
share, watch, and learn

Never be ashamed to take advice

Try not to nag

Laugh at work

Each day should be a lifetime

Do not cross the stream to find water

Through mistakes one becomes wise

Successful people are made not born

Avoid evil and it will avoid you

Actions are stronger than boasts

If you are going to have addictions, make sure that they are positive ones

Take care of yourself so you may help take care of others

Do less, be more

If something is good, let it be wonderful

Survival is a matter of instinct

You can accomplish a lot after a good night's sleep

Nature cannot be wrong

Tune your channel to creativity

Eat foods that boost your energy

Time and money are similar in at least one prime way: you should have fun with whatever is left over

Don't dish it out if you can't take it

Violence can never bring an end to violence

Kindness is dearer than gold

You'll make fewer mistakes by trusting other people than by distrusting them

Go as far as you can on the right road

Make the past your building block for the future

It is a mistake to avoid situations in which you might make a mistake

Love is something you give, not something you look for

Hard work never killed anybody

Remember that bad luck seldom lasts long

Every man has got to kill his own snakes

Live more good days than bad ones

Love while you are able to love

A day wasted is a day lost; a day lived is a day gained

Making a decision is usually a difficult chore

If you doubt an action is just, don't do it

Forget past disappointments

Chart your course well

Learn from others' mistakes

Think reasonably

It is more effective to do good than to preach it

Don't try live up to someone else's expectations

Reach down and lift people up

Keep your mind active and your life will always be exciting

Listening will enrich you much more than struggling to entertain others

Do not forget lessons you have learned

Having an opinion is the first step toward knowledge

Use the fact that human nature is impossible to change to your advantage

Moderation can be learned

You can do it

The deeper the foundation,
the stronger the house

A person who recognizes that
he made a mistake gains
intelligence

Abide at the center of your being

An old book is new to the reader who
has not read it

A dove has no place amongst
the crows

Doing things for yourself is not
wrong

If you will it, it will not remain
a fairy tale

Make the best decision you possibly
can at that particular moment

Possibilities are only realized when
action is taken

Love is a gift

A laugh is worth a thousand groans

Be content with little and your mind
will be satisfied

It takes a level head to win

Take it easy

You are as free as you want to be

Enthusiasm and passion are two
main ingredients for achievement

Every end is a beginning

Raise the bar in your life

Giving love is as much fun as
receiving love

Play while you play; work while
you work

The real test of business greatness
lies in giving opportunities to
others

Keep your soul young

One sincere apology is worth more
than roses

Never hide the truth

Thinking will always keep you busy

If you are silent, your integrity will
always be preserved

First be faithful and sincere

You are never older than you think
you are

If you lie so you do not hurt someone,
it is still a lie

Not everyone feels freedom in
a free land

Change the future

The easiest way to find happiness is
to quit complaining

Criticize the behavior, not the person

Do not start anything you cannot
finish

Happy people enjoy life more

The best time to prepare for old age
is when you are young

Remember each one of life's lessons
for a long time

Follow your own star

Make a difference

Exaggeration is usually done for
effect

If you look as if you own the world,
people treat you like you do

You win because you think you can

To control others, learn first to
control yourself

Play by nature's rules

A question you should often ask
yourself is, is it right?

Knowledge arrives from failed
experiments

There is no better looking glass than
an old friend

Implement your ideas

Sometimes by going slower, you
arrive faster

Be honest with yourself

Follow your own ideals and you can
never be called a coward

Memories are unrepeatable

Kindness always pays

See what happens when you agree
with criticism directed at you

Work should not be done for money
alone

Arrive at work early

Don't stand in the way of your own
    success

It takes thirteen muscles to frown
    and only two to smile

Great friendships go
    beyond words

Never go to bed angry

By speaking about your problems,
    some of them go away

Notice and celebrate daily miracles

Throw yourself out into the messy,
    wonderful world

You must empty the box before you
    can fill it again

Create a loving home

Listen to what people really have
    to say

Surround yourself with your own
    reality

Seek and ye shall find (Matthew 7:7,
    Luke 11:9)

Dig up questions by the roots

Live with he who sings and you will
    sing

We're all in this alone

Shun evil

Take time to live

Few wishes come true by themselves

Eat to please thyself, but dress to please others (Benjamin Franklin)

A good life is long enough

Do not go far from the ship or it might sail without you

You can tell a lot about a person by how he handles a rainy holiday, lost luggage, and a flat tire

Expect great challenges and meet them head-on

Develop yourself to your fullest potential

A little love goes a long way with a child

Slipshod methods bring slipshod results

Life continues to have value as long as you value life

Keep learning, earning, and yearning

Welcome the possibilities

Sometimes the times that scare you the most turn out to be the best times of your life

Don't forget the older people in your life

Figuring out the order of things makes everything a lot easier

To conquer fear is to summon wisdom

Make sure your ideals have foundations

It takes work to grow old gracefully

Most things that you worry about never happen

A person is a product of his words

Success is almost always met with envy

Never look a gift horse in the mouth

Stock up on friends; cut down on enemies

Give something back to society

Never make an enemy when you can keep a friend

Power enjoys the company of power

The smallest deed is better than the greatest intention

Everything is relative

The past is a great judge of the future

Love and work are two of the most important ingredients of a happy life

A leader is judged by his followers

Things happen to people when they are ready to let them happen

Some are born to greatness, some achieve greatness, and some have greatness thrust upon them (Shakespeare)

Believe until you find out otherwise

People tend to hate in others what they hate about themselves

Kindness begets kindness

You become what is in your heart

When you give to others, things come back to you

Fidelity to a worthy cause brings happiness

Give grief time to melt away

If you need an honest answer, ask an old friend

You don't notice little changes in people you see every day

If you want to do right, do little wrong

There is a foolish corner in the brain of the wisest men

Playing is one of the healthiest things you can do

You miss a lot of good things in life if you have the wrong attitude

Nothing matters very much and few things matter at all

Make happiness a habit

Make forgiveness a practice

You won't get if you don't try

Unite your mind and body

Character is revealed in moments

People despise what they do not understand

Understand the simple truths in life

Life isn't all beer and skittles (Charles Dickens)

Love obeys no master

If you can alter things, alter them; if you cannot, put up with them

Do not wait to start to living until you retire

Grow in consciousness

Make sure you can see the woods amid the trees

Promise little and do much

Vow to live fully in each moment

A change of scenery can spur creativity

Miracles occur when you least expect them

Kindness brings happiness

Your mind is an easy place to escape to

Let some things remain a mystery

The insolent have no friends

Improve yourself every way that
   you can

Devote your life to worthwhile
   actions and feelings

It is easier to forgive a child than
   an adult

Allow yourself to make mistakes

When you help someone because you
   love him, you are helping yourself

It is easier to *stay* out of trouble than
   to *get* out of trouble

We do not know who we are until we
   see what we can do

Learn to recognize the
   inconsequential, then ignore it

The only way to get the best of an
   argument is to avoid it

The most wasted days are those in
   which we have not laughed

You have no right to judge others

Forgive your friends

Get an idea, act on it

Laughter has no foreign accent

Sometimes, good advice is free and sometimes you get what you pay for

If you are not part of the solution, you are part of the problem (Eldridge Cleaver)

You can never be too gentle

Develop your compassion

Hope for the best

What you put into someone's life will someday come back into your own

Patience beckons inspiration

He who would not when he could, is not able when he would

In total darkness, a little light goes a long way

It is not enough to have a good mind; the important thing is to use it

Don't intrude upon a private moment

The energy we use in getting even might be used in getting ahead

Don't fix it if it ain't broke

Pay your bills on time

Small daily changes make life
spectacular

Greed lessens what is gathered

Never cast an anchor
in shifting sand

Having charm attracts
both men and women

Each person has a different capacity
for knowledge

Apologize in person

You become what you give your
attention to

Pass on insights that you have
discovered along your journey

Without passion, you cannot succeed

History teaches temperance

Don't conceal love

When you cease to grow, you begin
to die

You are meant to be very different
from everyone else

Seek solitude for growth

We criticize people we love more
than people we do not love

Enjoy learning for the sake of
learning

Make sure your hints are understood

Language is the dress of thought
(Samuel Johnson)

Go the distance

Don't compare your kids with their
classmates

Anticipation is greater than
realization

Life itself tends to explain life

Time waits for no one

It takes time to accomplish good
things

Don't be enraged when simple
irritation will get your message
across

Ask your purse what you should buy

Live for the present; plan for
the future

We are responsible for what we do,
no matter how we feel

When you have made a mistake,
admit it

Courage is the resistance to and
mastery of fear

The bridge you burn now may be the
one you later want to cross

Enjoy the struggle

Better late than not at all

Anger punishes itself

To get the full value of joy, you must
have somebody to divide it with

Procrastination is the thief of time

The best way to teach is by example

Without faith nothing is possible;
with it, nothing is impossible

Have your own private place to
which you can retreat

Little gear, less hassle

Take the time to express love

Make a secret wish

It is always your choice to view a
comment as insulting or not

Make sure your children are children when they are young

There is no true order for life

When you complain about your neighbor's faults, count ten of your own

Nothing great was ever achieved without enthusiasm

Make the complicated simple

Though we travel the world over to find the beautiful, we must carry it with us (Ralph Waldo Emerson)

Ignorance is expensive

Mirrors do not lie

Every great achievement was once considered impossible

Love many, hate few

If you want the rainbow, you gotta put up with the rain

Strive for perfection but do not become obsessed with it

The more ideas you have, the better

Always be in training so you perform at your peak

When you finish with a job, make the
  break completely

Stop getting in the way of your own
  success

If you think about the past too much,
  you may not enjoy the present

Keep the ball rolling

A happy person feels compelled to
  do more good things than a sad
  person

Enjoy the days that work out right

Don't lose the peace of years by
  seeking the rapture of moments

Just because some people are nice
  to you doesn't mean you should
  spend time with them

Figure out a way to enjoy life more

Always leave a room gracefully

If you truly love someone, you cannot
  be jealous of him

See a thing clearly and describe it
  simply

Never ask a barber if you need
  a haircut

Dramatize your ideas

A liar is worse than a thief

You pay for every lesson you learn

Saying something is the easiest way
to tell someone you are a fool

Making the right choices takes
a great deal of courage

You can always be more happy or
more unhappy

Feel more deeply the sweetness
of life

Being humble is a building block
to greatness

Do the hardest task first

A friend is a present you give
yourself (Robert Louis Stevenson)

One way to keep happy is to learn to
enjoy trouble

Enduring others' pain is easier than
enduring our own

There is a story in everyone's life

Discovery is seeing what everybody
has seen and thinking what
nobody has thought

Parenting is a profession

No one can make you feel inferior
   without your consent
   (Eleanor Roosevelt)

The past offers knowledge, the future
   offers hope

Heroes have flaws, too

Be better prepared than you need
   to be

What you give will afford you more
   pleasure than what you get

Keep your head

Never let the fear of striking out get
   in your way (Babe Ruth)

Other people's pessimism is a great
   fuel for your success

There will never be a better time to
   begin than right now

Find your own life interesting

If you miss the first buttonhole, you
   will not succeed in buttoning up
   your shirt

Look upon the errors of others in
   sorrow, not anger

Work hard because you want to, not
   because you are supposed to

Whatever you cannot understand,
   you cannot possess

To an optimist, every change is
   a change for the better

Cheer yourself up

Doubt is what gets you an education

Let your conscience be your guide

If you want to lose weight, eat less
   and exercise more

A man's home is his castle

Discover what you can do

Only a fool never changes his mind

Everyone in love is beautiful

Appearances can be deceiving

Bad television is a big waste of time

Give a civil answer to a civil question

Days should not pass without some
   laughter

A genius always thinks things can be
   done better

Your attitude is the first thing people
notice about you

Nothing is impossible

In the face of adversity, do not lose
your sense of humor

If you think too long, you may miss
an opportunity

The course of true love never did run
smooth (Shakespeare)

Young people have to be able to
make their own mistakes

Master your anger

Gain back your confidence

Let nature be your teacher

A kite rises against the wind

Work for companies of good character

Do not blame people for not feeling
the same way you do about
something

Don't wait for the verge of death
before you begin to live

Thoughts can make you more ill
than any virus

Never close the door on an opportunity

Education offers freedom

Face the consequences of your actions

Count all the good things that happen to you in a day before you count the bad things that happen to you

Too much bed makes a dull head

Get rid of everything that isn't good for you

Ignorance is the enemy of art

Don't believe everything you read

If you do not run your own life, somebody else will

Let your imagination work with no expectations

Don't deceive yourself

Make up your own instructions for life

Listen to what your body says

Don't achieve success at the cost of your soul

Love makes all acts more pleasant

Once in a while go someplace you've never been before

Never criticize with harsh intent

Set your own pace

The time to be alive is now

Kind people act kindly

Make yourself needed

Love is easy to spot when someone has found it

A parent can be tough and kind at the same time

Find your life's work

Things could be worse

There is no easy way to lose weight

Harmony is often obtained by playing second fiddle

Small steps are better than no steps

Don't jump to conclusions

Be willing to trust others

A good joke teller does not laugh while telling a joke

Separate yourself from the mob

Examine what you believe in

Nature is at its finest when you enjoy it

Dreams are your own stories

Laugh loudly

Break the habit of wasting time

If there were no problems, there would be no opportunities

Beat failure with courage

A place is as warm as the people who live there

Write letters

There is always a way

Look closely, lean forward, and just listen

Look at things in a new way

Anticipate trouble

Look for lessons others have to teach you

Recharge if you need to

Find the meaning in everything

Great men never feel great

Every day can be extraordinary

Pleasures change with the seasons

Art always reflects the artist

See problems as teachers and
opportunities for growth

Hatred is blind

The middle way is the best way

What you visualize, you can be

Even laughing at inappropriate
times is healthy

Always have your camera or you
may miss a good picture

Occupation can supply more
happiness than wealth

Manners are happy ways of doing
things (Ralph Waldo Emerson)

Be virtuous

Free yourself from anxiety

If you do not seize an opportunity,
someone else will

What's right isn't always popular
and what's popular isn't always
right

Begin new trails instead of following
old paths

A letter depends on how you read it

Discretion is the better part of valor

Seek respect

Money gotten the wrong way never
does any good

To achieve happiness makes others
happy

Spend a little time today for
tomorrow, but not too much
so that it ruins today

Rise early

Cleverness cannot take
the place of knowledge

A person does not become self-
confident overnight

It is better to work for nothing than
to be idle

Freedom brings peace

Some reasons are hard to understand

Life begins every morning when you wake up

Control your thinking

The higher you rise, the higher your horizon

Trusting in yourself brings trust to other people

If you cannot tell someone why you are mad at her, then you should not be mad at her

The only way to have a friend is to be one

Time treats everyone equally; so the question becomes, how do you treat time?

Four hands can do more than two

Growth demands a temporary surrender of security

History repeats itself because people have the same motives

Put your best foot forward

Listen to what people say in
conversations

Laugh away your sadness

Every difficulty in life presents us
with an opportunity to use our
inner resources

Excellence is its own reward

Ignoring facts does not change facts

Ideas can make the most dangerous
weapons

Give generously

Music begins where words leave off

A person who does not owe anything
is pretty well off even if he hasn't
got anything

Try not to bark up the wrong tree

There are no easy answers for
difficult questions

Always get back up on the horse

Never venture anything on a mere
possibility of success

Try honestly to see things from the
other person's point of view

Wait your turn

Nothing in excess

You can only die once for a cause

Anything you love is beautiful

Even people you do not know have an effect on your life

Talk is cheap

Win the last battle

A good storyteller can make a mundane anecdote exciting

The one who saves something has something

Happiness is hard to find in ourselves and impossible to find anywhere else

Our greatest joys and our greatest sorrows grow on the same vine

Buy low, sell high

Reflect daily upon the uncertainty of life

Give your child a slightly longer hug today

A genius needs to think differently
from the masses

Common sense defends the truth

Make full use of what happens to
you

When disaster strikes others it is
sad, but when it strikes you it
is devastating

No man is indispensable

Brush away criticisms made from
fears

Your mind can either free or
imprison you

Learn well and know better

The nature of things does not change

Lose no time

Always be employed in something
useful

Remember that everyone has
bad days

Admire people who succeed at living
life on their own terms

Apologize even if you win the
argument

Be independent

You must take the fat with the lean

By going slowly you sometimes
arrive faster

Work is love made visible

Success rarely comes without
a struggle

As new things succeed, old things
will die

You may have to forgo wealth and
power if you want to attain
happiness and freedom

Having money and truly enjoying it
requires a rare balance

Try to make a living engaging your
passion

Good enough is not good enough

You cannot live if you are always
sleeping

Fight for just causes

We are a result of what we've
thought

They stumble that run fast

Remember the whole when you look
at the parts

Teach your children to live their own
lives by living your own life

Where you live has a tremendous
effect on how you view life

The way to avoid great faults is to be
aware of little ones

It is easier to keep up than to
catch up

Most expectations cannot be lived
up to

You benefit whether you give or
receive love

Every path has a puddle

You can't help getting older, but you
don't have to get old

Perform every act in life as though it
were your last (Marcus Aurelius)

Making decisions is how we learn

You can always give a little more

The future should feel brighter than
the present

Don't let life feel like a burden

To hope is to live

Life has secret parts to explore

There is never an end to learning

A journey of a thousand miles must
begin with a single step (Lao-tzu)

The beginning is the hardest

There is no greater enemy than
yourself

Go to bed on the same day you
get up

There is no greater cure for misery
than hard work

You do not have to look a certain way
to be a good person

Confidence brings more to
conversation than does wit

Before healing others, heal yourself

Look within yourself and to your
family for entertainment

See reality

Words can be used as weapons

Let the other person feel that the
idea is his or hers

Love sees through a telescope,
    not a microscope

Use your time wisely

It is not enough to talk about or
    believe in peace; work at it

Your time will come

An open mouth invites a foot

Contentment is to the mind as light
    is to the eye

Time is a great healer

By improving your own life, you
    begin to improve the world

You cannot live without your dreams

Write commitments down

Every person is a volume if you know
    how to read her

In a united family, happiness arrives
    on its own

The best throw of the dice is to
    throw them away

Never despair

Don't change horses in midstream

Stick to the rule you laid down

Listen to nature; she speaks loudly

Keep the wolf from the door

Be part of the solution, not part of the problem

A good lather is half the shave

Seek first to understand

Try to live a great life, not just a good life

A lie usually causes more hassle than the truth

Rule your desires or they will rule you

If you cannot see the bottom, do not wade far

It is not enough for a man to know how to ride, he must also know how to fall

Retirement is a second chance to follow your dreams

Act with courtesy and fairness regardless of how others treat you

No matter what happens, you can still go forward

Charm only gets you so far

The sky's the limit

Do not get down on your job because
you are not quite up to it

Be democratic

Have grace under pressure

There is always something to learn

Usually people get the history they
deserve

It is well to give when asked, but it
is better to give unasked

Do not visit too often or too long

Being kind is more important than
being right

School teaches more than what you
learn from books

Do not open old sores

Most viewpoints should change
with time

Someone else's misfortunes are
easier to solve than your own

Appreciate beauty

Finish important, difficult tasks

Realize that every idea has already been thought of before

Mind your own business

Every heart has a secret

Failure isn't falling down, it's staying down

When you are through changing, you are through

Resist the urge to criticize

You can only learn to be a better writer by actually writing

Gardens can grow in tiny places

Love cannot take orders

Be absolutely determined to enjoy what you do

Carpe diem—seize the day

Sometimes a nap is the best medicine

Do not look too far ahead or you'll lose sight of the road

Each individual person only knows a fraction of what there is to be known

Happiness can only be found within

Avoid extremes

What you dream and imagine is
most real and creative

If you are happy here, you will be
happy there

Sometimes people take themselves
too seriously

Think as little as possible about
yourself

Live your life so that even the
undertaker will be sorry when
you die

An oak tree is just a nut that held
its ground

Look beyond your own interests and
be concerned about the feelings
of others

The good old days were never that
good

A house is not a home unless shared
with others

In difficult situations, think and act
like a child

Most things useful are beautiful

No one goes through life without
hurting some people

Fun is a safety valve that lets the
steam pressure off from the boiler

Visualizing love helps it take form

You should never be embarrassed to
learn something new

Those who cannot remember the
past are condemned to repeat it
(George Santayana)

The world belongs to the courageous

Freedom comes from seeing the
ignorance of your critics and
discovering the emptiness of
their virtue

Ingratitude is unpardonable

When you speak, offer data
and information rather
than beliefs and judgments

Cheap goods always prove expensive

It is natural for people to walk in
opposite directions

Caution is sometimes a hindrance

Be specific in your praise
and criticism

Knowledge also exists when you
know that you do not know
something

Dreams are a place to escape to

You can't achieve true happiness if
your goal is to show off

The degree of flattery should depend
on the strength of the person
being flattered

No task is overwhelming if you take
it one step at a time

There is no such thing as too much
style

There is a time to fish and a time to
dry nets

Adversity is never boring

To know what we know and to know
what we do not know—that is
understanding

It is easier to live without hate than
it is to live without love

You cannot tame life

Use the library

Too little and too much spoils
everything

Death is the great equalizer

Shake up your daily routine

Shun idleness

Knowledge is a stepping-stone to
the truth

Watch what you drink

Show more than just your age

The old have forgotten more than the
young have learned

It is a gift to lead a simple life

Do not interfere in others' quarrels

All things change, and we with them

Do not be afraid to let things
inspire you

The more knowledge retained, the
more power maintained

Common sense is the best kind of
intelligence to have

The best by-product of age is wisdom

The time to be happy is now

Perception is stronger than meaning

See what is all around you

One person's adventure is another's routine

Explode with joy

Part of getting well is having the will to get well

Choose worthy role models

Life should be looked at in more than one way

Try the ice before you venture onto it

Everything takes longer than you think it will

Remember that a person's name is to that person the sweetest and most important sound in any language

Do not shout

Changing yourself involves being open to your mistakes

Three things are needed for success: a backbone, a wishbone, and a funny bone

Make sure your time is valuable

You are never licked until you
   admit it

Receive praise gracefully

He who makes no mistakes, makes
   nothing

Plan prudently

Treasure your children for what they
   are, not for what you want them
   to be

If you thought about everything
   too much, you would never do
   anything

Little changes add up to great
   change

Give anonymously

Every day, look up one new word in
   a dictionary

There is more to life than increasing
   its speed

Find joy in everyday things

Trust your intuition

Be aware of your faults

When sick, create the best possible
   healing environment

If you think, then you are alive

Jot down what you are grateful for

People who need advice the most are the last to accept it

It is easier to be a critic than to be an artist

A man's fortune is in his own hands

Politics keeps comedians in business

Hold fast to that which is good

Haste makes waste

Never contradict your character to be fashionable

Keep the lines of communication open

Hear instruction and be wise

Wisdom helps us get through bad times and enjoy good times

A good book beats television any day

Ideas come from everywhere

Never dispute trivial things

Let truth guide you

Not everything involves money

In seeking to save another, beware
the risk of drowning yourself

Let the other person do more of
the talking

Life is too short to spend worrying

Simple things in life are usually
more satisfying

Let your dreams come from your
heart

Disaster is a good teacher

An intelligent person listens to
everyone and filters out what is
not needed

Making yourself less will never make
you more

As we live, so we learn

Find what matters

He who does not know how to serve
cannot know how to command

All of your feelings are acceptable

Rest makes rust

Make your reach exceed your grasp

Eventually time cheats us all

First come, first served

Live deep instead of fast

The more material things you have,
the less freedom you have

Embrace style, not fashion

Toss the junk mail

Invest in your health

Be prudent

Soak up each day like a sponge

If you want a place in the sun,
you must leave the shade of
the family tree

Be good at living life

Do not be afraid of defeat

Act with all your might

We are individually responsible for
our lives

A person's wisdom gives her patience

Avoid drawing conclusions

Bugs beget bugs

It does not profit you to gain the
whole world but lose your
own soul

Nothing is good or bad but by
　　comparison

Take a chance on the young

Kindness is the oil that takes
　　the friction out of life

You can't say yes to everything

Treasure your spouse

No harm in trying

Tell others when you admire them

No person goes through life without
　　experiencing some tough times

Have your imagination

Perfection only exists in our dreams

Don't bet anything you cannot afford
　　to lose

The truth shall make you free
　　(John 8:32)

It is seldom the fault of one when
　　two quarrel

Challenges make life interesting

Stand on your own two feet

Many things take practice before you
　　get the hang of them

Schedule time for daily reflection

The test of the heart is trouble

Pain occurs when pleasure is absent

Progress always has a cost

Every minute counts

He who bears the burden on his shoulders knows its weight

A gentle disposition will, with application, surmount every difficulty

Create and then follow through on the creation

Character consists of what you do on the third and fourth tries

Remarkable achievements begin as thoughts

People are more attractive when they are hard at work

Foolish people think good ideas are foolish

Silence is the best expression of scorn

Age is a thief

Philosophy is about hope

Happiness is where you find it

Starve a fever and feed a cold

Carry spares

Think like a professional athlete

Win arguments by forgiving

How you treat your children will be reflected for generations

The more people who are doing well, the better it is for everyone

Get lost in books

Look on the bright side

Show up to defend yourself or you risk being presumed wrong

People may doubt what you say, but they will always believe what you do

You are the master of your fate

Think of what you have instead of what you want

Don't let others determine your thoughts

Do not make excuses; make good

People in love are not afraid

If you want to be loved, then love

Meet your own needs

Remember the important moments in life

Losing desire is like losing your life

Appreciate the good others do

If you want to get promoted, do things to get noticed

Don't ever wish failure upon someone

A teenager is learning all the lessons you already know, for the first time

Being happy does not have to be expensive

Don't ask for too much

Spend more time as a participant in life than a spectator

It takes all kinds of trees to make a forest

Life always goes forward

Understand that young people must play and laugh

Don't complain

It often takes more courage to change one's opinion than to stick to it

A load becomes light when cheerfully borne

Never let the past vanish

Talk out bad feelings

No one can make you feel bad without your help

Character is what you are in the dark when no one is around

Happy people change what does not make them happy

Don't kindle a fire you cannot extinguish

Make something happen quietly

Politics is the only arena where telling the truth can ruin a career

Take some time off

Observations are a part of experience

Learn to type

You can catch more flies with honey than with vinegar

Prosperity is appreciated more in the wake of adversity

Opportunities rarely come in neat, predictable packages

Understand how you learn best

If you cannot believe everything will turn out for the best, then at least believe that things will not turn any worse

If you have one true friend, you have more than your share

Pamper yourself now and then

Look for friends who share your outlook on life

The smallest details, when cared for lovingly, can add up to a masterpiece

Look for the order in life

When you hear an ambulance, say a prayer

A patch is a sign of thrift;
a hole is a sign of negligence

Make life less difficult for others

Look beyond people's behavior to
what good they can do in life

The way to become boring is to say
everything

What you don't ask for, you don't get

Don't waste your time on lousy books

You lose a lot of time hating people

No great advance has ever been
made without controversy

Superficial friends offer superficial
help

The only way to save an hour is to
spend it wisely

Limit the number of irons in your
fire

Exercise your human will

Swing for the fence

Eat, drink, and be merry

Do not underestimate your enemy

The only goal of any political party
should be to make things better

The more knowledge circulates,
the more it increases

Hate less

If you borrow trouble you'll pay
a high interest rate

Make your good points outweigh
your bad ones

A full cup needs a steady hand

Holding on to fears gives them power

When sorrow comes, remember that
you have experienced joy and
will again

You can't change your spots

Keep your mind busy

There will always be another
opportunity

No is more easily changed to yes
than yes to no

Give as you would receive: cheerfully,
quickly, and without hesitation

Don't tear down the east wall to
repair the west

Progress begins with dreams

Visualize your goals in order to achieve them

Know what you can control and what you cannot

People are as happy as they make up their minds to be

Only two things are infinite: the universe and human stupidity

Using the right word makes all the difference

A strong foundation can handle many earthquakes

Cure grief with action

Find out what you are made of

Craving more things takes away from enjoying what you have

Treat yourself to something on your birthday

Life is a comedy for those who think it is funny

The longer you stay in one place, the greater your chances of disillusionment

Silent company is more healing than words of advice

Let memories strengthen you

A sign of strength is knowing when to stop

Get good directions before heading out

Whatever catches our eye long enough will catch us

You may house your children's bodies but their souls are their own

Walking can be a moving meditation

Excise the word *bored* from your vocabulary

Liberty can be preserved with education

Stick with your family

Want what you have

Say "thank you" when complimented, nothing else

It is easy to convince someone to do something when it is what he wants to do

The eyes give away how you feel

Do not burn any bridges behind you

Froth is not beer

It is not selfish to love yourself

Remember that you become what you practice most

When you are eighty you will want to do the things that you were able to do when you were seventy

Talk in terms of the other person's interests

Fond memories make growing older more pleasant

A person's true character comes out in an argument

Keep your faith in good friends no matter what they do

Success is never attained through mediocrity

Forget about the Joneses

Wisdom takes hard work to acquire

Many small opportunities added up equal as much as one big one

Knowledge can take you further than anything else

If you want to know about a child, observe how he plays

Give others opportunities to be generous

Some people would still not be happy if they had everything, while others would still be happy even if they had nothing

Use your mind as a tool

Comedy is simply a funny way of being serious

Getting older and living for a long time are two different things

What is well learned is not forgotten

When you are passionate about things it shows

Your imagination can set you free

Surround yourself with talented people

Even natural abilities need cultivation

First impressions aren't everything

People who hate others, hate themselves

Do what you must and do it well

Never play without a contract

Refrain from defending your
reputation

Walk away from temptation

Do not keep love secret

Strive for excellence, not perfection

If counting to ten does not ease
the pain and anger, then count
to one hundred

Change the current of your thoughts
if they distress you

Say positive things to people you love
every day

Heaven helps those who help
themselves

If you have a job without
aggravations, you don't have
a job

Enjoy your children even when they
do not act the way you want
them to

In every victory, someone is hurt

Think before you speak and act

Greatness relies on the ability to
make the right decisions

Travel to broaden your mind

Read the dictionary

Appreciate your circumstances

Truly happy people don't brag

He who lives in the present,
lives in eternity

Action is eloquence (Shakespeare)

Give things time

Keep your attention on what is your
concern

Don't keep people waiting

A parent needs to be more
disciplined than the child

Doing beats stewing

Never threaten if you can't follow
through

Meditate in your own way

If you know you're going to lose,
do it with style

Look for the niche in life that will
make you the happiest

Send energy into your life

Be true to yourself

The difference between books and
television is in the way we use
our imagination

Nobody is all wrong

People tend to put burdens on
themselves

You don't need the answer to all the
questions, only which questions
to ask

Reach for things that are beyond
your grasp

Life is not a problem to be solved but
a gift to be enjoyed

Look at Earth as a spacecraft and
you the explorer

Wrong is always wrong

If you wish a job was through,
do it now

Don't throw out the baby with the
bathwater

Music creates mood

Life is a great teacher

Look for the ridiculous in everything and you will find it

True love takes patience

Don't cheat

If you think twice before you speak, you will find that about 90 percent of the time you will have no occasion to say a word

Your age is in your imagination

Reading great books makes you smarter

Ambition is the incentive that makes purpose great and achievement greater

Too much comfort weakens the mind and body

Do not interrupt others or finish their sentences

People watching is an art and an education, not a science

It is our attitudes and reactions that give us trouble

Nature will take its course

Do not look for home atmosphere at a hotel or hotel service at home

Define yourself as a person, not a job

Searching for meanings lasts a lifetime

Abstinence is the best medicine

The brain works for you even when you are at rest

Don't start economizing when you are down to your last dollar

The work is never done

Whatever you want, want it more than anything

The sun is always shining someplace

Talk sweetly

The less you want, the more you have

Your marriage is okay when you can still make up after an argument

When children stand quiet, they have done some harm

If you try to please all people, you will fail them and you

Don't walk when others stop

Be grateful when you're feeling good

That which had no force in the
beginning can gain no strength
from the lapse of time

Live a life well lived

Life is a daring adventure

Take a walk every day

Don't major in minor things

Brooding over blunders is the biggest
blunder

The remedy for an injury is to
forget it

Free yourself from fear

Half our mistakes in life arise from
feeling where we ought to think,
and thinking where we ought
to feel

Learn to know when you are well-off

Love works wonders

Remember your goals

Let your hair down

Support what you feel is right and oppose what you feel is wrong

Retirement should be the first step toward a new life

Little children have big ears

A good teacher is a master of simplification

What good parents instinctively do is always best

If you want something, you have to make the effort to get it

When trying to be helpful, focus on little things

Play an active role in your child's education

Don't be afraid to think

Follow through on good ideas

Patience conquers life

Be humble and polite

A little step taken may be the beginning of a big journey

Don't take good friends, good health, or a good marriage for granted

A friendship that can end was never
   really a friendship

High places have their precipices

Make sure your conscience is clear

The limited are the only ones that
   see limitations

Worrying wastes a lot of time

Envision what you want to be,
   then be it

Modesty is praised; arrogance,
   reviled

Believe nothing unless it agrees with
   your own reason and common
   sense

Accept pain and disappointment as
   part of life

In nature, nothing is done without
   a purpose

Making time is an art

The best time to get started is
   the present

Little is needed to be happy in life

When death finds you, be doing
   something that you love

Good words are worth much and cost little

A person can do a lot of things if she has to

Even art is not perfect

It is not what you are, it is what you do not become that hurts

Enjoy that two people can have entirely different opinions while looking at the same thing

What you do between birth and death is up to you

Other people can help lift you to a higher self

Beware of the person who has nothing to lose

Mind the store

Stick to your goals

Content yourself with being a lover of wisdom, a seeker of truth

The more you put into a thing, the more you get out

Teachers open the door, but you must enter yourself

Limited funds are a blessing,
   not a curse

Clarify your expectations

Necessities before luxuries

Aging does not have to be a difficult
   process

Love can make it all right

A good marriage is made up of two
   good people

Never do anything against
   conscience

Be your kids' best teacher and coach

Take the initiative and
   play your game

A rainy day makes a sunny day all
   that much more enjoyable

Liars are usually good at their trade

Make your life meaningful

Patience will achieve more than force

Be confident that you are
   making good decisions

Jealousy cannot live in love

Death is only felt if it is feared

Listen to people who are good
　　listeners themselves

Say what you think

One hour of thinking may equal as
　　much effort as five hours of
　　physical labor

In realizing that we do not have all
　　the answers, we find humility

Opinions change with age

Expect happy endings

Old age is a time for understanding,
　　not regret

Love is about beginnings

Don't get upset by small things

Allow yourself to be imperfect

Share your wisdom

Aim high

Every little bit helps

Do not judge a person by his opinion
　　of himself

In truth lies wisdom

Put up with small annoyances to
　　gain great results

Don't give up or give in

Never underestimate the intelligence
of your opponent

Dream for a living

You can never really win an
argument with a child

Do not let someone else's reality
become yours

Adults lie more than children

Occasionally it is okay to throw out
the to-do list

Search for the truth in others'
opinions

Napping prepares the mind for fresh
thoughts

Examine all ideas

Be content regardless of the presence
or absence of material success in
your life

The wonderful thing about saints is
that they were human

Give spiritual strength to others and
they will reciprocate with
affection

Make history your teacher

Adopt good habits

Let each part of your business have its time

The greatest use of life is to spend it on something that will outlast it (William James)

Plenty ought to be enough

The best things come in small packages

He who only hopes is hopeless

The best ingredients make the best meal

A smart mouse has more than one hole

When you are in the wrong, you cannot afford to lose your temper

Perfection is never necessary

Happiness is meant to be shared

Avoid making too many changes at once

Choose doctors who treat both the patient and the disease

He who demands does not command

Remember to say thank you

Row your own boat

Never let the irregularities of your own life be the subject of your discourse

Trust the facts

Don't let your possessions possess you

Nothing in life is to be feared—only understood

Learn more than you are taught

Be spontaneous

Hard work inspires creativity

The best way out is always through

It is easier to admire someone you do not know well than someone you know well

Serve others as much as possible

There is a lid for every pot

Life is easy when it is simple

Leaders are always out in front

Silence cannot be misquoted

Remembering life can be as pleasant as living it

If you don't know what to do, don't do anything

Love is the best inspiration for the arts

You can disagree with someone and still love him

Don't lecture someone after she apologizes

Follow your visions

Take the dare

Give yourself space to breathe

Good words cost nothing

Only you know the reasons of your heart

Age is only important if you are cheese

Never hesitate to answer when a child asks "why"

Use common sense to make better choices

Don't tolerate foul language

To learn from history, study it

Hear more than what you understand

Don't make excuses

Sometimes even a good thing can appear bad

Better safe than sorry

After clouds, clear weather

Practice forgiving

Keep trying, no matter how hard it seems; you will get better

Sometimes a truth should not be told

Don't brag about one child in the presence of another

Look for the innocence in people

Be master of the mind rather than be mastered by mind

In an orderly house, all things are ready

Challenge life

You can't steal second if you don't take your foot off first

The trials we endure can and should introduce us to our strengths

Don't humiliate another person

Fearing death is a waste of time

Drop your superstitions

Look for ways to praise others

The body has a miraculous capacity to heal itself

Leave some time each day for introspection

Keep track of your successes

Your friends have an effect on your destiny

If you can't come by something honestly, you are better off without it

Stay busy and accomplish much

Your thoughts affect your health

It is not how you arrive at the truth, but that you get there

A person who has a match will find a place to strike it

Laugh at life more than cry about it

Build castles in the air, then put
   foundations under them

Emit positive energy

No revenge is more honorable than
   one not taken

Love can make it all worthwhile

Even when you are sick and
   depressed, love life

Break free of bad habits

Small changes add up to a big
   change

Not everything should be said

Enjoy patience

It's always something

The great mind knows the power
   of gentleness

Physical beauty doesn't last

Be lovable

Excuses fool no one

Keep your sense of humor

A fire is not out until the last spark
   is extinguished

Fortify the soul

Sometimes you can't find a reason

Highs are better after lows

It is never too late to learn

A job is what we do for money; work is what we do for love

What counts most is what you have under your hat

Unlearn procrastination

Safeguard your reason and it will safeguard you

Always be honest with yourself

One man's trash is another man's treasure

Greatness cannot be faked

Never tell yourself you cannot do something

Use your public library

Keep good company and you'll be counted as one of them

Better let someone else act foolishly than you

Risk failure

Errors start from truths

If you do not understand something, do not dismiss it as useless

Become more appealing

Everyone has at least one great idea

Be a student of life

It's no good running if you're on the wrong road

When you talk to someone, figure out whether she wants to listen or talk more

Your intuition is your instrument

Doing something right is reward enough

Everyone excels in something at which someone else fails

Act as if you were already happy and that will make you happy

Save money

Life divides people into two categories: those waiting for something to happen and those making something happen

Balance your life

A simple life is elevated

If heaven is your goal, then no ascent
   is too steep to accomplish

Get rid of all but one or two credit
   cards

The effort can be more satisfying
   than the goal

Let inspiration come from within

A good remedy for anger is delay

The time is always right to do what
   is right

Never abandon certainty for hope

Be happy and your children will be,
   too

Love goes where it is sent

Advance in learning as you advance
   in life

Beware of little expenses

Do not slouch

Volunteer

The world is your stage

Change your thoughts and
   you'll change your mood

Sometimes competition is not
appropriate

In order to be successful, you must
fail first

Don't let your sins always be
the same

Never take advice on childbearing
from someone who does not have
children

True love cannot exist without
friendship first

Look on the sunny side

Praise loudly; blame softly

Love has a life of its own

Knowledge is power

Find fun where you can

The more you have, the more you
want

Never underestimate the influence of
the people you have allowed into
your life

Paint like you feel

Do not let your nights go into days

Those who think they cannot are
generally right

Do not let makeup hide your beauty

Everyone must row with the oars
they've been given

True generosity is the ability to
tolerate ingratitude

A mean-spirited adult was probably
a mean-spirited child

Hope is especially important when
there's nothing you can do

Worry's best antidote is action

Let life happen

The secret of success is consistency
of purpose

Fear is the energy to do your best in
a new situation

Value your good health

Sometimes it is difficult to choose
between knowledge and
ignorance

Trust kids to do as much as they can
on their own

One hand washes the other

Don't follow the wagon tracks
   too closely

Learn from the mistakes of others
   because you cannot live long
   enough to make them all yourself

Give yourself a day off

Knock and it shall be opened for you

Honor in love is silence

Children can be very cruel

Conduct yourself with dignity

Live long; live well

Thinking too much is the major
   cause of missed opportunities

There are no sure things in life

Self-trust is the first secret of success

Too many pleasures often lead
   to pains

Don't leave until you know where
   you are going

Cope calmly to achieve inner
   serenity

When things go wrong, don't go
   with them

No kingdom divided can stand

Listen to your body's signals

People listen to wealthy people more often than to poor people

Scrambled eggs cannot be unscrambled

You are what you are when nobody is looking

It pays to advertise

Forbidden fruit is sweetest

Get to know your neighbors

No place is as happy as a home with love

Life is too short for us to spend all of our time trying to figure out why we are here

We must face what we fear

Where do you want to go today?

Abusive language is abuse of language

Smile as much as you can

Choose the way that seems the best, however rough it may be

It is better to give than to receive

Be your unique self

Better to be useful than popular

Something is better than nothing

Faithfulness to duty brings rewards

No one has a right to coerce others

Help a friend in need before he asks

It is not the load that breaks you, it is the way you carry it

Look for opportunities to show praise and appreciation

You begin to understand parental love when you become a parent

Your imagination can take you to great places

In times of great stress or adversity, channel your anger and your energy into something positive

Nurture your talents

A lie can never become a truth

Changing along with life's cycles takes preparation

Master the fundamentals

You should tell your child she is doing a good job before she has to ask

New life is everywhere you look

Enforce family rules

Laugh it off when someone does not like you

There is always an easier way to do it

When you are too busy for your friends, you are too busy

Beware of too great a bargain

Do not let money own you

Think today and speak tomorrow

Your brain needs exercise to stay fit, just like your body

Open new doors when old doors close

A cow must graze where it is corralled

Use your own definition of success

Spare moments are the gold dust of time

Defeat the fear of trying

Humor makes all things tolerable

A wise person never thinks that he is wise

One simple touch can have more impact than a thousand words

Excise debt

An open heart receives love better than a closed one

Observe proportion and moderation

Have the stamina to meet obstacles and overcome them

Peers are the greatest teachers

Everyone has time if she cares to make it

Take in life cheerfully

There is nothing to be gained by wishing you were someplace else or waiting for a better situation

Higher price doesn't necessarily mean higher quality

Elevate relaxing to an art form

A person must risk something of significance in order to achieve something of significance

Everything has its price

A great marriage does not bind the two people but sets them free

Never argue with someone who talks loudly

We all have our blind spots

A home without books is like a house without windows (Henry Ward Beecher)

Never take sides when your friends are upset with each other

Successful communications must flow in two directions

Ideas need fertilizer in which to grow

Charm can be used as a key

Be polite to beggars

Anger profits nobody

Life is a game to play

Do not rely completely on any one person

We can grow in spite of our pain or, perhaps, in response to it

Trust, but verify

Kidding around often indicates
a want of understanding

Love makes sense to the two people
involved

You're going to spend the rest of your
life doing something; it might as
well be something you want to do

Double your joy by sharing it with
a friend

Being in love changes everything

Gather the roses of life today
(Pierre de Ronsard)

Develop your imagination

Know your shortcomings

Whatever you're worrying about is
probably not as big a deal as you
think it is

It is impossible to know what it is
like to be anybody else except
yourself

Liberate your soul

Home is a spa for the soul

Go through life feeling neither greed
nor envy

Bring adventure to others' lives

Try to come out of terrible experiences stronger

You only go around once

Learn to enjoy silence

Call attention to people's mistakes indirectly

It is more courageous to live than it is to die

You can keep going long after you think you cannot

Stay interesting

Trace your family tree

Do what needs doing

A child needs love most when he deserves it the least

Unless you repair a crack, you will have to rebuild a wall

Recharge your life by taking one step each day

Whatever you have, spend less

Take things always by their smooth handle

Complacency is more persuasive
than anger

Knowing why you are intimidated
can give you the edge

Summer definitely has a gentler pace
than any other season

It is too late to learn how to box
when you are in the ring

Try to incorporate the qualities of
your heroes and heroines in
your life

The best remedy for a dispute is to
discuss it

Genius is thinking in an unusual
way

Don't say no till you've heard the
whole story

Life requires our full energy

Sometimes the world isn't ready for
certain ideas

To climb steep hills requires
a slow pace

Happy people think happy
thoughts

All our dreams can come true—if we can have the courage to pursue them

Patience is often better than medicine

If you cannot afford to do certain things or buy certain things, don't

Desire and aversion, though powerful, are just habits

Become aware of your moods and how to change them

People who can take advice are sometimes superior to those who give it

When you've reached your goal, then tell others about it

Never shut the door on learning new things

There is no need to yearn, envy, or grab

Leave a good impression on people

Life is learning how to put principles into practice

Things may not be what they seem

Fame usually comes to those who are
thinking about something else

Practice breathing until you get
it right

Help and share with others

Ending up with anything valuable
takes time

Character and hard work go together

He who plants kindness gathers joy

Without passion, nothing is worth
doing

Look back on the progress of
your life

Pay attention to what is good for
yourself

Don't let the tail wag the dog

Lost innocence and wasted time are
never recovered

A gold cage is still a cage

Integrity is the best mantle

Let sleeping dogs lie

It pays to believe in miracles

A few words can mean more than
a whole book

Try to do the things that you know in
your heart are right

Orders are orders

Given enough time running water
can hollow out a stone

Share the remote control

Art is long, life is short

Life's journey is more pleasant if you
choose the right companion

Do well with your time here

Most people know their own faults,
so it does no good to alert them
to them

If you get caught in a lie, it will be
assumed that it is not the first lie
that you told

Every time you go to complain,
stop yourself

So little is said of what could be said

Marriage is about communications

Choose the right moment to make
your move

Attention is the mother of memory

Listen to the things your child
 does not say

Honesty leads to greatness

Sometimes you have to go looking
 for luck

You are born to succeed

One leg cannot dance alone

Be brave and you will find strength

Never give up on the possibility of
 happiness

Listen to your critics

You can never go wrong by searching
 for the truth

Strive for a balanced life

Your wants should be easily supplied

You do not have to be in prison to be
 a prisoner

Opportunities are made not found

Be and do and dream of the best

Underhanded practices fail in
 the end

Do not write before your pencil is sharpened

There is no rose without a thorn

Admit to your mistakes

Solving problems keeps you young

Love affects all ages

Beware the fury of a patient man

Mind your P's and Q's

The purpose of history is to teach

Each bird likes his own nest best

Question what others accept

Nature does her part; you have to do yours

Each day, do something good for yourself

Cynicism can make anything look foolish

Giving up your youth does not mean giving up your life

Health is never an issue until someone gets sick

Surround yourself with people, colors, sounds, and work that nourish you

Make the most of what you've got, what is actually yours

Spread happiness

Growth requires you to learn new habits

Thinking is always free

Youth is a once in a lifetime opportunity

Know your situation well

The more you "stretch," the more you can fit in

Treat everyone you meet like you want to be treated

Have sweet dreams

Over time, many problems resolve themselves

It is easier to criticize others than it is to criticize ourselves

If you reveal a weakness, it can become a strength

Don't knock it till you've tried it

Make yourself necessary to somebody

Fear of being alone creates more marriages than love

Don't compromise your integrity

It is never too late to mend

If you do not look out for yourself, nobody else will

Take care of your loved ones

Any publicity is good publicity

A true genius says and thinks things for the first time

If you cannot sleep because you're worrying about work, then you are in the wrong job

Don't wait until the last minute

If you work eight hours a day and sleep eight hours a day, that gives you eight hours to do whatever you want

Achieve luxury without debt

You do not have to eat the whole tub of butter to get the taste

Stay ahead of the pack

Sometimes it is difficult to see the wisdom in things

Give because you want to touch someone

Judge and you shall be judged

Don't wage war to achieve peace

Feel your thoughts

You control each new day

Don't let fear hold you back

Reexamine your assumptions

A poor excuse is better than none

When it rains, look for the rainbow

Our lives are lit by millions of kindnesses small and large

Don't stop until you are done

It is harder to live with fewer rules than with many

Pluck is better than luck

Survey and test a prospective action before undertaking it

If you leave your place, you lose it

Busy people have more fun

Make little decisions with your head
and big decisions with your heart

Live wisely, well, and justly

Every time you forgive someone, you
strengthen yourself

People hate most what they envy
most

When the door is shut, the work
improves

In the long run, compromise will get
you more than stubbornness

Examine life

An alarm clock may wake
you, but you have to
get up yourself

Diligence is the mother of good
fortune

Humor can be a vehicle to saying
something serious

Start your day with the most
important thing you have to do

Oversleeping will never make your
dreams come true

Put your money in trust

What you truly need is usually
within easy reach

In marriage, a person has to live
with twice as many faults

The toughest thing about success
is that you have got to keep
winning

When you get on first, make your
goal going to second

Make adjustments as you go through
life

Be prepared for emergencies

If you are willing to admit when you
are wrong, you are right

In time, the truth always comes out

A problem adequately stated is
a problem well on its way to
being solved

Thinking is the greatest amusement

Keep several irons in the fire

There is no way to happiness;
happiness is the way

Don't play with your food

Always stop to think when your fun
will cause another's unhappiness

If you would not write it and sign it,
do not say it

Get out of your own way

The secret of patience: do something
else in the meantime

Take care of what you have while the
world lets you have it

Face up to your responsibilities

Joy is an achievement; you earn it

Develop a strategy for a good life

Add little to little and there will be
a great heap

Starting a task is half the battle

Think innocently and justly

Sometimes you need to lose in order
to win

Real talent is never foolish

Start living your ideals

Conform your wants and
expectations to reality

Don't talk about people behind their backs

Don't be a martyr

If we take care of the earth, it will last a long time

A thought can be right, but the argument wrong

Always accept an outstretched hand

The person you love ought to know it

Life is a loan, not a gift

Peers persuade the best

He who would climb the ladder must begin at the bottom

Make the best of a bad situation

Almost everything looks better after a good night's sleep

Suspect everybody—and keep your suspicions to yourself

Exercise your brain

He who judges others condemns himself

No news is no news

An honest confession is good for the soul

Watch what works with other people

Thoughts should not be punished

Never deny the truth to yourself

Put your principles into practice

Pursue your passions

No one is infallible

Know when to be silent

Inner beauty will last longer than physical beauty

Ideas go through life cycles

Friends deserve leniency

Do things only for people who want things done for them

Don't interfere with things that don't concern you

The reward of love is love

Faith is the vision of the heart

You can't beat winning

Imagine yourself in the other person's shoes

Good books have good readers

Quality shows

Refuse challenges to fight

Grow old in body only, never in mind

Sometimes you have to lose everything before you can find what you want

A little leak will sink a big ship

Never underestimate the power of a kind word or deed

Open your eyes and see things as they are

Old age is a victory, a privilege

Play it close to the vest

Challenge each of your handicaps

Be happy for successful friends

Moral progress results in freedom from inner turmoil

No matter how long or how short you are alive, live well

Patience is bitter, but its fruit is sweet

Every argument has at least two
points of view

A small gain is worth more than
a large promise

Opposition should not be taken
personally

In a fight between you and the
world, bet on the world

Avoid melodramatic reactions

Let the other person save face

Love is the glue that holds
a marriage together

The only time a woman really
succeeds in changing a man
is when he is a baby

Planning your future saves you from
regretting your past

By helping others, you will feel good
about yourself

If you do what you've always done,
you will get what you have
always gotten

The road up may be the same road
down

Start living your ideals

If you grasp something, you will
  lose it

Time reveals all the answers

You should not always bail your
  children out of trouble

Learn as much as you can from as
  many different people as you can

Don't take politics or business
  personally

Material wealth does not equate
  success

Eat less, live longer

Honor your father and your mother

Liberty, like charity, begins at home

Volunteer your time

When there is something unpleasant
  to do, do it first

Stay curious

You eat the fruit of the tree
  you plant

Time avenges all wrongs

Wear clothing that fits

Pretending to be perfect is
exhausting

Never forget the debt you owe to all
those who have come before

Don't change everything in your life
at once

There's a fine line between good
and evil

A criticism is only an opinion

Thinking is one of the hardest tasks
you can do

You can't get wool from a frog

Story can take us far beyond fact

Letting anger out leaves room to let
love in

Great achievements are always
possible

Every man has a price

He who hurts, gets hurt

Be disciplined

Don't keep your prized possessions
hidden from the world

Civilization begins at home

Knowing what to forget is just as important as knowing what to remember

Special things done in excess no longer remain special

Practice will drive what you become

You are in control of how you respond to the behavior of others

We get what we give

Most new ideas are just old ideas recycled

Before you buy shoes, measure your feet

Don't rejoice when your enemy falls

Start your own world

Live with grace and intelligence, bravery and mercy

Think seriously before responding to provocation

Knowledge takes away mystery

There is always more to life than what you see

Think big thoughts

Don't trust your memory; write it
down

Avoid negative people, places, things,
habits

Wait for the right moment

Nature moves slower than man

Always keep exact accounts

Put your knowledge to its full and
good use

Revel in nature

Do not let your genius be the same
as your flaw

Let go

We cause things, both good and bad,
to happen in life

It is not what you have, but how you
use it

Appreciate it when you see
something unique

If you don't know the answer, say,
"I don't know"

One must see a hazard to avoid it

Desire keeps the economy going

Keep your fears to yourself, but
    share your courage

When joy comes, celebrate it

You create your own future

Live by nature's rules

Better on time than late

Know thyself

Confidence outweighs good looks

Wisdom is revealed through action,
    not talk

Successful people are successful
    because they think that they are

He who does evil usually suspects
    others of evil

You can't make an omelet without
    breaking eggs

Bite the bullet

It is better to have a little than to
    want a lot

Never doubt your abilities

Give what you have

The surest cure for vanity is
    loneliness

Leave the world a better place than
it was when you arrived in it

Support a charity

Inspiration will find you if you start
doing things

Find pleasure in your looks

A walk helps the inside as well as
the outside

It is easier to be generous than
grateful

Every pea helps to fill the sack

If you wish to know the nature of
a man, place him in authority

The clock will always win in a race
against time

Regained freedom is appreciated
the most

It is the mind that makes the body

See the miracles that happen
every day

Where there is life there is hope

Take the scenic route

It is a rare thing to win an argument
and the other fellow's respect

Many a heart is caught on
the rebound

Living is succeeding

Liberty is not license

Don't eat before you set the table

Heroes die too

Don't rob Peter to pay Paul

Try harder

An enemy will agree, but a friend
will argue

Do it your way

Education finds truths

Home is where you act the worst and
are treated the best

Few blame themselves until they
have exhausted all other
possibilities

If the shoe fits, wear it

Don't just grab the first thing that
comes along

Don't approach a horse from the rear

Suggest what is right, oppose what is wrong

You cannot know too much, but it is easy to say too much

Be a thoughtful friend

The guest of the hospitable learns hospitality

He is no man who cannot say no

After a game a player's character is revealed as much as during it

Delight in the simple things

Keep your desires in check

Take charge of your attitude

Spring always arrives after winter

Be contented with what you have

Do not hold anyone else accountable for your shortcomings

Keep quality in your life

Accept more praise than criticism

There are a lot of bumps on the road to easy street

The best way to handle any crisis is to remain calm

The best times are had with family and friends

Don't be afraid to ask for directions

Anger is often more hurtful than the injury that caused it

Faith laughs at impossibilities

Make people feel special by thinking about them

Overestimate travel time by 15 percent

A little absence does much good

No one else can be another person's savior

Cheerfulness, helpfulness, and honesty are good companions to take with you through life

Respect—and demand respect in return

You cannot find happiness unless you search for it

Never apologize in entertaining

Every man must bear his own burden

It is impossible to defeat an ignorant man in an argument

Talk in deeds and actions

Experience pleasure in your own company

Instead of generating, take in

Do a good job because you want to, not because you have to

Know when to be quiet

When life hands you a lemon, make lemonade

You will never know until you try

Live all your days to the hilt

One doesn't know knowledge, one acquires it

Make your life, do not copy it

If nature is a giant canvas, then life is the artwork on it

Don't talk about your diet

Sight and insight are requirements of a good life

Time flies when you're having fun

Do not light your fire until you have gathered your sticks

A sleeping cat cannot catch a mouse

Happiness is often the result of being too busy to be miserable

Life can be so complicated and busy that sometimes we forget to live

Do a thing and have done with it

Save time for thought

Assume that everyone else is doing the best he can

Hope gives a person strength

Don't bore people with dramatic stories of your exploits

There are two kinds of people: those who have ideas and those who do something about them

You control yourself

Don't hurt yourself and don't hurt others

Great friends are for great occasions

Be an honest person and you'll be regarded as one

Imagine what you would attempt to do if you knew you couldn't fail, then do it

There's always room for improvement

Row away from the rocks

Other people experience the same level of grief as you do

Get the other person saying "yes, yes" immediately

Set things in order

Relearn an old skill

Quality is more important than quantity

The first step is the hardest

Faults are thick when love is thin

Fear springs from ignorance

Remember the simple pleasures of being a kid

Laughing makes you live longer

You'll never grow old if you continue to think and learn

It is not enough to be busy

Being too sane is worse than being
    a little crazy

Right will triumph over might

If you can't think of someone
    lovingly, better not to think
    of him at all

Lend only the books you don't care to
    see again

Adventure is never risk-free

The world owes no man a living

Keep your words soft and sweet; you
    never know when you might have
    to eat them

Experiencing things makes
    them real

Motivate by example

Cultivate the tree that you have
    found to bear fruit in your soil

When a child speaks, really listen

To lock up mischief, keep your
    mouth closed

Most of our troubles come from
    within

Don't cross the bridge before you get there

Very few things happen at the right time

When you can't solve the problem, manage it

The thing that often occurs is never much appreciated

The secret of business is to know something that nobody else knows

The world will always get better

Remember the dignity of simplicity

What we think is who we are

An opportunity is hidden in every adversity

A gift with a kind word is a double gift

Both sides benefit in a good business transaction

Old age should be a new experience

Proper praise sticks

Stop blaming others

Action is worry's worst enemy

Painful truths should be delivered in
the softest terms

Spontaneity is not a virtue in and of
itself

After you've worked to get what you
want, take time to enjoy it

You can't try to do things, you simply
must do things

Believe the best of everybody

Do not throw away the old till
you know the new is better

Inaction saps the vigor of the mind

You can do anything in your dreams

Industry keeps the whole body
healthy (William J. Bennett)

Without the past, there is no future

Avoid sarcasm

Vote in every election

Opportunity does not
knock the door down

You do not have to slow down just
because you get older

If you care, it will show

The sooner the departure,
the quicker the return

Listen to your feelings

It takes courage to attempt new
things

You do not have to be blind to not see

Wisdom spurs happiness

Nine-tenths of wisdom is being wise
in time (Theodore Roosevelt)

Once you taste losing and survive,
trying in the future becomes
more comfortable

Power seldom brings happiness

There is nothing so fatal to character
than half-finished tasks

Cherish solitude

Bring your cooking to an art form

Don't argue with people whose
opinions you don't respect

Luck doesn't make you smart

Let knowledge grab you

Keep track of your life by writing in
a journal

Make your life more exciting than
your dreams

Knowledge is more valuable than
money

Let no one see you in a hurry

You cannot love a pet too much

Within each person is a treasure, but
sometimes you have to dig for it

Learn from failures instead of
brooding over them

The manner of giving is worth more
than the gift

The faster you get information,
the faster you think you need it

Family stories keep families alive

Admit ignorance; seek knowledge

Sometimes you need to create
a new life

What you are good at never seems
hard

If you think you cannot, then you
will not

Don't pay for work before it is completed

In a battle, the heart will win over the brain

Your happiness is the result of your own effort

As a cure for worry, work is better than whiskey

Every job is a self-portrait of the person who does it

Washing your face and hands will refresh you

Stick to one thing until you get there

Set television rules

Only those who have the patience to do simple things perfectly will acquire the skill to do difficult things easily

Being less pessimistic is better for you than being more optimistic

Passion cannot be substituted

Find expression for a joy and you will intensify its ecstasy

Much can be completed in the time it
takes to gossip

Try something different

Develop the skills you need to move
forward

Don't provoke the rage of a patient
man

Good actions give you strength and
inspire good actions in others

In any project, the important factor
is your belief

Record your beliefs

The respect others give you
determines the value of
your advice

Pay yourself first

Attempts to control everyone and
everything are fruitless

Many will forget the past for
a present

The great challenge of life is to
determine what's important

You never get something for nothing

The young should be taught, the old should be honored

Keep birthdays simple

Write in your heart that every day is the best day in the year (Ralph Waldo Emerson)

Play your cards well

Be virtuous, and you will be happy

Taking a step back is sometimes the best way to continue forward

Selective distrust is the parent of security

Look the person in the eye when you say you're sorry

Live so that expenses will not be greater than earnings

The world you live in is created by your mind

Remember the influence of example

Obligation can turn into hatred very easily

Learning to live is learning to let go

Failing means something just did not work

Life is what we make it

Get smarter as you get older

Continue to do the things that have
made you happy in the past

An action that does not proceed from
a thought is worthless

Rule yourself

Celebrate your nonmaterial assets

Adopt the patient pace of nature

Lighten up

Risk begins from within

Pleasures last a lifetime

Some people find faults even with
vacations

In order to truly learn, one must put
away all preconceived notions
and be open to exploration

Most folks are about as happy as
they make up their minds to be

Pleasure is more intense after pain
or hardship

Being able to forget is as important
as being able to remember

Don't assume you're always going to be understood

Everything has an end

Learn something new every day

Don't allow yourself to be pulled down by someone who is depressed, hurt, or frustrated

Accomplishments are the ornaments of life

The true measure of a person is how he treats someone who can do him absolutely no good

It is easier to blame than to praise

Do not let other people's judgment influence your judgment of other people

Love is the best companion for sorrow

The mind is designed to be able to expand

Good criticism is very rare and always precious

People are disturbed not by the
things that happen, but by their
opinion of the things that happen

It all depends on how you look at it

A weak foundation destroys the
superstructure

A healthy person is a successful
person

Truth keeps the hand cleaner
than soap

Straighten up your room first,
then the world

If you don't know, know where
to look

Live beneath your means

Say hello to others

When you go to bed, don't worry
about problems

Don't shout dinner until you have
your knife in the loaf

The only way to never get
disappointed is to expect nothing

It isn't the mountain that wears you out, it's the grain of sand in your shoe

In order to be happy, you must be able to laugh

A sense of humor reduces people and problems to their proper proportion

Being nice does not cost anything

Happiness comes from within and relies very little on exterior things

Do not push your luck

Before you act, consider the end

It is easier to change than to change back

Accidents happen

A pearl is often hidden in an ugly shell

The past cannot be improved, but the future can

The heart that loves is always young

It is not fair to ask of others what you are not willing to do yourself

Be willing to change a little

Other people's adventures can be inspiring

Write down the things that interest you

Be flexible to changes in your plans

Truth is usually available to the seeker

A bold attempt is success

Find the uniqueness in each individual

There is no better time for beginning

Live for the present and future because you do not have the power to undo the past

Don't be in a hurry to tie what cannot be untied

A kindness given to one person is contagious and will be passed along

A town is only as good as its people

Take more pictures of people than of places

Expect big returns in life

When in Rome, do as the Romans do

The ripest fruit falls first

Start each day with a clean slate

Maintain a sense of perspective and proportion in all your endeavors

Take one step at a time

A true genius makes the complex understandable

Keep renewing yourself

All great things had a small beginning

Exercise with a partner

Do what you need to do to make the best and wisest use of your time

Fear is a powerful force

Turn your limitations into beautiful privileges

Those who bring sunshine to the lives of others cannot keep it from themselves

Nothing can make a person happy but what comes from within

You can successfully battle and
overcome difficulties

Don't take yourself too seriously

Children should not be used as
status symbols

Go a little past your comfort zone

Take refuge in your mind when you
need it

Set up clear, consistent, and fair
rules for kids

If it isn't broken, improve it

All ideas are possible

Avoid making idle promises
whenever possible

A tree falls the way it leans

To be angry is to punish yourself for
another's sin

Love gives you the strength to start
over again

There is only one way to tell
the truth

Life should be ruled from within,
not from without

Absence makes the heart grow fonder

Cause gives a person strength

You can only be sure of today

Free yourself from the confines of self-absorption

The more content you are with yourself, the fewer material things you need

You usually know the right thing to do; the hard part is doing it

Perseverance can do many things genius cannot

Consider things from every angle

The audience makes the show

Believe in others and they'll believe in themselves

The world needs great ideas for simple problems

If you think about it too much, you will never do it

Learn from the mistakes of others as well as your own

In every enterprise, consider where
  you will come out

Gold is where you find it

If you live fearing death, then you do
  not live

Good fences make good neighbors

Reason above everything else

Contemplate the beauty of the earth
  and find reserves of strength that
  endure

When you accept a task,
  finish it

It takes something to create
  something

All time is of equal value